ESSAYS ANCIENT AND MODERN

The Rev. Fr. Donald A. Dodman, L.Th.

Copyright © 2013 by Fr. Donald Andrew Dodman
All rights reserved.
For information visit: www.donalddodman.com

Manufactured by Createspace.
Cover art by Devan Alexander Burnett

ISBN 978-0-9810750-3-7

ACKNOWLEDGEMENTS

Devan Alexander Burnett
For Everything

Other Books By Father Dodman

A PRIEST'S TALE: Autobiography of a Gay Priest - 2008
TROUBLED SEAS - 2012
DEATH IN THE RECTORY - 2012

PROLOGUE

ONE
The Pentateuch   9
Reflections on the Pentateuch   31

TWO
The Doctrine of Man   49
Reflections on the Doctrine of Man   73

THREE
The Doctrine of the Church   101
Reflections on the Doctrine of the Church   123

FOUR
The Nature of the Eucharist   153
Reflections on the Nature of the Eucharist   175

FIVE
Faith and Works   193
Reflections on Faith and Works   201

SIX
Clerical Celibacy   219
Reflections on Clerical Celibacy   233

SEVEN
The Oxford Movement   249
Reflections on the Oxford Movement   277

EIGHT
Duncan and McCullagh   293
Reflections on Duncan and McCullagh   319

EPILOGUE

PROLOGUE

March 2012

The final year of my divinity studies was a tutorial, or graduate year, styled after the Oxford model. There were no lectures, save for Greek classes, and the week was spent reading and gathering information on a particular, predetermined subject. My method was to jot notes on index cards as I read so that when it came time to write I could shuffle the cards according to a schema of what I wished the paper to accomplish.

On the Thursday evening of the week I would then type the paper directly from the information on the index cards, which would then be read to my tutor on the Friday morning. It will undoubtedly be obvious that the writing in the original essays is somewhat rough and unpolished as they were simply intended for oral presentation. Questions and discussion would follow the presentation. This Tutorial Year occurred during the academic years 1967-8.

One of the essays I include here was actually a hand-in essay written during my first year of Theology and involves the origins of the core material of the Old Testament. The Pentateuch paper was intended to be an introduction to themes in scriptural study, which would follow through all of the ensuing studies and be an introduction and a basis upon which the whole biblical framework would stand. Aside from that one essay, the others all date from the final tutorial year's work.

Interestingly, the professor who read and graded the Pentateuch paper wrote several comments on those pages, which I will touch upon in due course. (One of his comments, I had not really fathomed until I revisited the essay recently in preparation for this volume.) Otherwise, the presentation of all the subsequent papers was made orally to my tutors.

Concerning my attitude and approach to Holy Scripture, I suppose the fact that I came from a background with no defined religious input, I was more or less a clean slate, devoid of preconceived ideas. I was aware that many Christians held to an inerrant concept of the Bible. Even so, I realized there were many questions and mysteries that would need to be pondered carefully. Hence, the seminary experience for me was truly a process of growth and development.

During the course of the Tutorial Year, some 200,000 words were written and from the thirty or so papers produced, I have selected eight to form the focus of this discourse. They seem appropriate to me because they act as a springboard directly into many issues and problems, which now have a currency that has captured the church and the religious and social concerns of the twenty-first Century.

It must be remembered that I wrote these papers while a young seminarian almost 50 years ago. I propose to respond to certain points in each of the essays from my present perspective. Undoubtedly, it will be noticed that my thinking has changed considerably in many respects because of the ongoing development of theology and a good dose of experience, including my realization that the real world does not always work out as neatly and cleanly in practise as it might on paper.

I chuckle to myself now as I contemplate how I used to think, in the days of my youth and self-righteousness, that Bishop John Spong was a heretic, having myself been nurtured in a somewhat sacrosanct Anglo-Catholic tradition. Now I am even possibly further afield from the accepted track than he. It makes me all the more appreciative of the open-ended and *outside the box freedom that is the spirit of Anglicanism.*

Some of the discussion to come relates to various breaks in communion over the centuries in the Churches of the East and West. Currently, there is almost daily news of new divisions within the Anglican world. Historical and theological issues have become obstacles between Christians—literalism and concepts of the meaning of life and of the vocation of the Church are still in conflict. There appears also to be the unfortunate process of *dumbing down* thinking in the Church today, which places theology in a precarious position and in fact probably accounts for much of its failure to engage discerning people.

It is ironic that Canada was instrumental in bringing about the first Lambeth Conference of Anglican Bishops in the late 1800s. Bishop Colenso of the Diocese of Natal in Africa was at the centre of a controversy as he tried to cope with a realistic and pastoral view of human sexuality with regard to the issue of polygamy and the baptism of converts in his part of Africa. The present day conflict, which seems to be focussed very much on African ideals and the development of contemporary thinking in both Canada and the US, is also preoccupied with similar issues, but in this case the tables have been reversed as it were.

It is the height of irony that it is now Africans who are fussing about these ostensibly core issues and it is now the West that is struggling to bring a more inclusive demeanour to the Church. That theme will be expanded in one or two of the reflections to come.

My original papers were produced on a very heavy and ancient Underwood typewriter—my pride and joy which I purchased for $35 in 1965 when they were becoming redundant in the world of business. It was a beautiful piece of machinery. I no longer have it as it was wrecked in a car crash I was involved in on my way to my first parish appointment. In the original manuscripts I had to hand write in any Greek and Hebrew notations. In this edition, I of course have the luxury of having fonts on my computer to fit almost every occasion. I do not intend the Greek and Hebrew words to be a distraction to anyone, however to some readers it may be of interest. In any case, I have ensured that there are transliterations in Roman letters for those particular concepts. One additional note: Only that one essay (on the Pentateuch) was a 'hand-in', so instead of trying to deal with footnotes here I have taken the liberty of incorporating such references into the body of the text itself as was typical in all of the orally presented tutorial papers.

One will undoubtedly note that in the old essays the practise was then to capitalize words like God, Church, Sacrament, Bible and so on. I am now following a more current convention, as there might be no end to what could be considered sacred or profane, although I do keep to using a capital for God and a few other concepts where it is appropriate. Likewise, the modern practice of using the pronouns He or She for God, which in so much literature today can be an irritating distraction to smooth reading (e.g. S/he, or She/He), I have simply avoided doing that with the caveat that whenever I use a personal pronoun for God—whatever that might be—it means the all inclusive and infinite God. "It", a neuter pronoun, would be totally inappropriate when referring to God who we hold to be personal yet without sexual identity.

I trust that the reader will find the development of my thought over the years to be compatible with the developing motion of theological study.

Donald

ONE

THE PENTATEUCH
Old Testament I
Oct. 25, 1965

The Pentateuch is a term used to denote the first five books of the Hebrew Bible. This name comes from the Greek, meaning "five-rolls" or "fivefold Book". These five books are Genesis, Exodus, Leviticus, Numbers and Deuteronomy. Early rabbis often refer to the Pentateuch as the "Five Fifths of the Law", an indication that the fivefold division is not a recent invention. Another term that is often used to denote this section of the Bible is the "Torah"--(teaching or instruction). Pentateuchal literature can be classified or broken down into two main divisions, 1) History: from the beginning of things with the Creation story up until the time of the Israelite encampment on the plains of Moab. 2) Law: the book of Leviticus contains nearly all the material that is legal in nature.

Exodus and Numbers contain a combination of law and history; Deuteronomy consists mainly of addresses involving the law to a great extent; Genesis, even though it is chiefly narrative, mentions law concerning marriages and the Sabbath given in very early times, and also laws governing food in the days of Noah.

Another term, which is invariably associated with any study of the Pentateuch, is the word "Hexateuch". This term refers to the first six books of the Bible—the Pentateuch plus the book of Joshua. Joshua, because of its contents and literary structure is intimately linked with the Pentateuch. This book describes the final stages in the history of the origins of the Hebrew nation.

MOSAIC AUTHORSHIP

Moses was born, as nearly as scholars can ascertain, around, the year 1520 BC. He is reported to have been 120 years old at the time of his death, (Deut. 31:2.) This would indicate that he and his people left the land of Egypt around the year 1480 BC, during the reign of Princess Hatshepsut. During the sojourn in Egypt, of Moses and the Israelite people, c1520-1480, the Egyptian throne was occupied by Thotmes I, II, and III successively. Josephus, in one of his histories, mentions the name of the Egyptian princess who supposedly found Moses in the reeds—Princess Thermuthis— a very close resemblance to the name Thotmes who would have been on the throne at that time. Princess Hatshepsut, who had adopted Moses and taken him in like a son, died at almost the same time that Moses and his people fled from Egypt. This to some seems to be a rather noteworthy coincidence.

There is some evidence that the Hebrew people were connected with the mines in the land of Midian near Egypt. In one of the Temples in that area Sir Flinders Petrie, in 1904, found evidence of burnt sacrifices indicating that perhaps the Israelites had worshipped there. Egyptian religious ceremonies and customs had nothing corresponding to this. Also, the temple was equipped with small stone altars used for burning incense as the Hebrews had done for centuries. The Egyptians also burned incense but this was usually done in metal receptacles. Another feature of the Temple of Serabit, which reminds us of the religious practises of the Israelites, is the ablution basins. (Ex, 30:18 and 19.) We are also reminded of Jacob's dream and the pillar, which "he set up... and poured oil on the top of it". (Gen. 28:18.) In the Temple of Serabit there were found several stone pillars that quite possibly could have been used by the Israelites. No comparable idea is found in the Egyptian religions.

Other interesting aspects of this study, which would lead to the conclusion that the writer of the Pentateuch was familiar with Egypt and with desert life, are his knowledge of the Egyptian language, and of Egyptian customs. The writer seems to have an ability to transcribe Egyptian names into the Hebrew language with great accuracy. Such names as Pharaoh, Potiphar, Asenath, Zaphnath-paaneah, Push and Shiphrah show very little evidence of Hebraizasion in form. The probability of this having happened through an oral tradition by people unacquainted with the Egyptian language is highly unlikely. Also, anyone other then a first hand witness would have made many mistakes or would probably not have given finely detailed descriptions such as we find in the Pentateuch. We are given a very accurate picture of life in Egypt in the story of Joseph. The moral standards of the Egyptian aristocracy of that age are typified by the attitude of Potiphar's wife when she attempts to persuade Joseph to be a "little more" friendly. We find that on a 19th Dynasty papyrus there is recorded an incident almost identical to this one, and it is told in a very blasé manner with not a hint of surprise or shock—as though it were an everyday occurrence. Another piece of evidence indicating that the writer had an intimate knowledge of Egypt is the situation reported in the King's dream in Genesis 41:17. "Kine coming up out of a river, and feeding on its sedgy banks, were a common enough sight in Egypt, but in Canaan must have been unknown."'

The mention of seven-eared wheat also typifies the awareness of Egyptian life, for such a variety of wheat is nowhere mentioned in connection with Canaan or the surrounding countries. Joseph, when he was called up before the king of Egypt, first shaved and changed his clothes. Such a practise in Israel, it is claimed, was not followed, For example in II Samuel 10:45 we find this:

> "So Hanun took David's servants, and shaved off half

the beard of each, cut off their
garments in the middle, at
their hips, and sent them away.
When it was told David, he sent
to meet them, for the men were
greatly ashamed. And the
King said, "Remain at Jericho
until your beards are grown,
and then return."

In the narratives concerning the Exodus we find many more instances of customs and cultural habits, which were common to Egypt but rather unknown in the land of Canaan.

In Exodus 5 we read of bricks being made with mud and straw. This was the practice in Egypt but not in Canaan. In fact to make bricks without straw had become an aphorism for something that was impossible. Also in Egypt the practice of reaping near to the ear of the corn and grain was uncommon in the land of the Israelites. The Israelites were used to tying the grain into bundles or sheaves instead of collecting it in baskets, as many Egyptian monuments seem to suggest.

PLAGUES

The order in which the various plagues struck the land of Egypt is another point that would lead one to assume that Moses, (or at least the writer of the Pentateuch), had a good knowledge of the life of Egypt. The first plague was the turning of the Nile into blood or at any rate the discolouration of the water.

This event is assumed by many to have happened about the beginning of July when river was rising, (Ex. 7:19) The frogs, which came next, are usual in Egypt in the month of September.

Lice, which some people conjecture could possibly mean mosquitoes, would have been next in approximately October. November and December would have been the time for the plague of boils to strike.

This has been connected by some scholars with diseases of cattle. The plague of hailstorms would coincide with the usual storms and general poor weather of February in Lower Egypt. Plagues of locusts have been common in March and May and the last pestilence, the "Darkness, which might be felt" seems to possibly have been the desert storms, which are common at that time of year. (Much of this material is discussed in George Warrington's book, When Was The Pentateuch Written?)

In musing about their life in the land of Egypt, the Israelites remembered quite accurately many of the fine points of their sojourn there. In Numbers 11:5 we read, "We remember the fish which we did eat in Egypt freely, the cucumbers, and the melons and the leeks, the onions and the garlic." This is a very accurate appraisal of the type of diet, which would have been common among the lower classes in Egypt at that time. Vegetables such as these are mentioned nowhere else in the Bible. Not one of the common foodstuffs of Canaan such as honey, milk, figs, raisins or olives is included in this list.

The journey of Moses and his people through the wilderness also attests to the familiarity of the writer with the countryside and the various other aspects of desert living. Descriptions of many of their places of encampment can to this day be identified because of the accurate detail even though knowledge of the place names has passed into antiquity. In Numbers 33:9 we find such places as Marah, Elim, Dopkah and Rephidim. Maps have even been reconstructed from Biblical information plotting the journey of the Israelites. Such an accurate knowledge of these places presupposes a first hand account, for tradition would never have preserved the detail.

Reference in the Pentateuch to distance is another measure of the accuracy with which the author is writing. Moses speaks of a "three day journey" to the wilderness from Egypt. This length of time would appear to be approximately correct for such a journey, however one who had not actually been on such a journey would hardly have been able to reconstruct the details with such accuracy. "It is most improbable that tradition should have handed them (the details) down so accurately." (G. Warrington.)

There seems to be throughout the Pentateuch, and indeed throughout the whole Bible, a firm faith in Moses as the author. This is a very widely held traditional opinion, Even our Lord referred to the Pentateuch as "the Book of Moses". (Mk 12:26) In the second Epistle to the Corinthians the Apostle Paul says that Moses "is preached and read". (2 Cor. 3:15) Again, the evangelists make reference to "Moses and the prophets" in Luke 24:27 and our Lord Himself in Luke 16:29. Moses, says Jesus, in John 7:19, "gave the law". Throughout the Old Testament we also find a good deal of evidence to support the general belief that Moses not only gave the Law but that he committed it to writing. Malachi 4:4 is a good example of this. "Remember ye the law of Moses my servant, which I commanded unto him in Horeb for all Israel with the statutes and judgements." Also in Ezra 3:2 we read of the building of the altar and the establishment of the ritual "as it is written" in the law of Moses. Daniel is but one other who backs up this theory that Moses was the actual author of the written law. The bearing of the Ark by David, to Zion was accomplished "as Moses commanded". (1 Chron. 15:15)

There is much evidence in the Old Testament to indicate that the Israelites are very familiar with the life of the desert and with life in an alien country. The Hebrew nation was prohibited from following the ways of the land of Egypt and for that matter from the ways of the land of Canaan to which they were going. (Lev. 18:3). The laws of the Pentateuch, it is claimed, must have been written down in the Mosaic period because otherwise had they been passed on in the oral tradition they would have been modified and adapted to agree with their new way of life. Their form of expression would most likely have changed.

Another argument that would support the view that the Pentateuch was committed to writing at a very early date is the one that argues that the understanding of the doctrines of the future life, the Messiah, angels and worship are more primitive. Compared to other Old, Testament literature we can readily see that the Pentateuch is from a much earlier date.

ARGUMENTS AGAINST MOSAIC AUTHORSHIP

Until the time of the Reformation there was very little concern about whether or not Moses had written the Pentateuch. It was almost universally assumed that Moses was the author. In the eleventh century a Spanish Jew, Rabbi Isaac ben Jasos, pointed, out that the founding of the Hebrew monarchy must have been much earlier than the account of it in Genesis 36:51. Another man, Ibn Ezra, in the twelfth century found certain references rather difficult to reconcile with Mosaic authorship. A learned scholar,

Andreas Masius, claimed that the Pentateuch was put into the form we now have it by Ezra or "some other" man of God. The first man to notice that there were two main streams of writing in Genesis was Jean Astruc, physician to Louis XIV and professor of medicine in Paris. He did not claim that there were two authors but rather that Moses had probably used several literary sources. Astruc noticed that one of these authorities consistently used Elohim for the Divine name and the other used Jahweh. He thought that Moses, after having completed Genesis, then went ahead and wrote the other four books. After Astruc came many, many scholars who took and developed this theory much further.

In the ensuing years many theories were proposed to explain the complex facts that had come to the surface. One of the first theories to be developed was known as the Fragment Theory. This was because in the Pentateuch there are many pieces of writing in which no continuity or order could be traced. The train of thought seems to change without notice from narrative to law to history in the middle of books. The next system was called the Supplement Theory. In this one the use of the word

Elohim for God is thought to be the main body of writing and the oldest literature. It seems to have a common plan throughout. The writer who is often called J or the Jahwist then annotated and added new sections. Deuteronomy was considered to be the most recent addition to the Pentateuch. In 1853 Hupfeld discovered a second Elohim source and so the Document Theory was born. This was really a modification of the Supplement Theory. It was based partly on this find of another Elohim source and partly on a better understanding of the "literary layers" of the Pentateuch. The word "Document" was used to name this theory because it was believed that four independent existing documents were the basis for the Pentateuch as we have it.

Scholars have used the letters J, E, D and P to represent these four documents. J or the Jawist document relates incidents before the call of Moses. It uses the name Jehovah or Jahweh to designate God. The Elohistic document, E, intertwined with J, uses the Hebrew word Elohim to mean God. D is used to indicate the work of the Deuteronomist. This person's work comprises the greater part of the book of Deuteronomy. P represents the Priestly code. This source includes history and law, written from the Priestly point of view. Many scholars believe that these four sources in turn came from some preexisting oral or written source. H. K. Graf was a student of Edward Reuss and Julius Wellhausen. The work done by Graf and Wellhausen is quite significant to higher criticism. Their special contribution in this work is the chronological dating of the various strains of writing. They would place the documents in the following order —J, E, D and P. Most scholars would tend to agree with this order although some insist that E should be dated before J. These four sources can be placed according to date roughly in the following periods:

J	about	850 BC
E	about	750 BC
D	about	650 BC
P	about	500 - 380 BC

(Some scholars prefer to give dates that are somewhat earlier than those cited above.)

The document called J can be seen all through the Pentateuch, and E is interwoven with it. D is chiefly found in

Deuteronomy and P apparently has served as a final pattern for the whole compilation. In the time of Josiah the Book of the Law was not in the Pentateuch, as we know it today. The developed Pentateuch grew and blossomed during the centuries following Moses. The use of the Divine Names Yahweh and Elohim have from the beginning of this inquiry into higher criticism been the focal point in the separation and unravelling of the strands.

In the account of the Creation in Genesis 1:1 – 2:4 the word Elohim is used 55 times and Jehovah not at all. We find in Genesis 2:4-25 a combination of both these names. In Gen. 2, the second account of the creation, Jehovah is used 27 times and Elohim not at all. Thus, we see that the theory of two distinctly different strains of authorship is based on reasonably solid ground. In the two accounts of creation we see two somewhat varying portrayals of Man's corruption and God's consequent displeasure. There are also two accounts of the entering of the ark; the rising of the water; the perishing of all living things and the drying of the earth. We find a disagreement in mathematics over the period of precipitation. One account reports 40 days and the other 150 days.

One version states that only one pair of each species was taken into the ark and the other that seven pairs of clean animals and one unclean were accommodated. The story of God's announcement that Sarah would bear a son for Abram also has a second form found in Genesis 17 and 18.

Moses' own father-in-law bears two different names in two places, Exodus 2 and 3. It does not sound very likely that a man who could remember details so well would forget such an intimate detail as his own father-in-law's name. Likewise, there are two accounts of the sending of quails and manna, Ex. 16 and Numbers 11.

Even in the legal sections of the Pentateuch there seems quite a difference of opinion on many questions. In the Covenant, sacrifice can be offered anywhere as long as the altar is made of earth or unhewn stone. Deuteronomy plainly and emphatically states that sacrifice is not to be offered in local sanctuaries. (Deut. 12, 14 and 16. The Book of the Covenant knows no priestly race—priests can come from any of the tribes and even heads of families are allowed to offer sacrifice. In Deuteronomy we discover that this has been somewhat limited to only the tribe of Levi. Even a third view is offered by the Priestly code; only the sons of Aaron can offer sacrifice. This means that only a particular branch or family within the house of Levi could perform the functions of the Priesthood. (Exodus 28 and Numbers 3:5-10.)

We find that there are also differences in theological conceptions among the various strains of authorship. This is quite evident in the two accounts of creation. In the second account, which is thought to be the earlier one, we find a very primitive and anthropomorphic God. He 'fashions' man, and 'breathes' life into his nostrils; 'takes' a rib and 'builds' the rib into a woman. He 'plants' the garden and 'sets man down into it'. This account is very different from the other which is much shorter and seems to stress the word <u>create.</u> This is somewhat more theologically refined. The J document often explains events by working into them a touch of the miraculous. One also feels that the writer of J is trying to sway or aid God in His decisions. God is a much more sophisticated God in E. He does not appear in human form but reveals himself to men through dreams and through the ministry of angels.

The general tone of J and E is prophetic. In E there is much less evidence of conscious ethical and theological thinking. Deuteronomy, or D, has its own particular attitudes a well. The prohibition of worship at local sanctuaries (mentioned above) is an outstanding idea peculiar to Deuteronomy. This legislation was made to curb the worshipping of "many Jehovahs" as had become the fashion at that particular time. There are many, many peculiarities of language, vocabulary and usage among the various sources. However, a sound knowledge of Hebrew is really necessary before one can discuss these subtleties intelligently.

In the P document the anthropomorphic ideas of God are much reduced. There is no mention of dreams or angels and the writer' outlook is rather narrow in scope. Religion to him is apparently to a large extent ritual and form. It is certainly at variance with J and E. There is a sharp distinction between the Priests and the Levites.

If the whole of the Pentateuch is a patchwork, and not just Genesis as Astruc thought, then Mosaic authorship is almost unthinkable. Many passages imply that they were written after Moses' death, the notable one being, of course, the actual announcement of his death in Deut. 34. Many passages refer to Moses in the third person. Geographical terminology in many places cause some doubt to arise. The often used phrase "beyond Jordan" would imply that the author lived to the west of the River. This would not be true of Moses. A post Mosaic date for the authorship of the Pentateuch would also be assumed by many other references.

Gradually the body of literature, (poems, epics, sagas and law), was modified and supplemented until a new, up-to-date code of ethics and morality was arrived at—a code that would suit the advancing and developing Hebrew nation. The Pentateuch reached its completed form most probably before the year 400 BC.

CONCLUSION

In searching for a rational and honest view of the place of the Pentateuch, one cannot help but feel that those who radically oppose any type of analytical research are beating a dead horse. Their methods do not seem to be based on a scientific or logical approach. Only facts in favour of Moses' authorship are taken into account and far too much time is spent trying to shoot down the opinions of other scholars rather than in developing concrete and positive evidence of their own. So many of the people who oppose the use of higher criticism seem to be terribly afraid that once they discredit any piece of scripture the whole of it will fall to pieces before them. On the other hand we can perhaps take the higher criticism approach to an extreme and do almost as much injustice to the Pentateuch. One can get to the point where the analysis becomes rather ridiculous and perhaps something of a fad. Dillman, as quoted in James Orr's book, The Problem of the Old Testament, makes this intriguing remark, "with a Q1Q2Q3 (=P), J1J2J3, E1E2E3, I can do nothing and can only see in them a hypothesis of perplexity."

It is usually very easy to make rash and final statements about the things we feel strongly about. Here I quote two such statements: The first is from The Bible, its Origin, Its Significance And Its Abiding Worth, by A. S. Peake.

> "So far we have reached two results. One is that the Pentateuch is composed of various documents, the other is that it cannot be the work of

Moses, but must be much later than his time."

And from George Warrington in his book <u>When Was the Pentateuch Written?</u> Who says that he "would not be the least bit surprised if the actual stone tablets that God etched "with His own finger" were not uncovered at any time".

Surely somewhere between these radically opposed views there is a position that may be very near the truth. Perhaps an actual man named Moses did take an instrumental part in the initiation of the works we now call the Pentateuch, but surely it is plain that the Pentateuch has been added to and enriched by many people.

REFLECTIONS ON THE PENTATEUCH
March 2012

Some of my earliest memories of the scriptures are of my maternal grandmother reading bedtime bible stories to me. They were from some sort of collected and simplified stories rather than from a bible as such and the pages were augmented with many dramatic, engraved pictures of the characters from the stories and of vivid depictions of the Creation, the Flood, the Crossing of the Red Sea and a host of biblical themes.

Grandmother was some sort of evangelical Christian even though I remember having been given the Prayer Book with which she was presented on the occasion of her confirmation in the Church of England when she was a teenager. Apparently, in the early years when they had first immigrated to Canada, my grandparents dabbled in some other unorthodox organizations including the Jehovah's Witnesses. Actually, it was so far back in history that the organization was then known as *The Bible Students* and there was frequent talk about a Judge Rutherford who headed the organization. Apparently, the group experienced a number of splits and those who had been known as Russellites eventually evolved into the Watchtower Society and renamed themselves Jehovah's Witnesses. By the time I came along Grandma and Grandpa had separated so I never knew them as a family, but rather as two individuals who were never seen in the same place at the same time, making for an awkward family situation.

At that age—three or four years old—I had absolutely no preconceptions or opinions about religion and I simply enjoyed the stories as pleasant bedtime reading on the weekends I stayed over at Grandma's house. I gave no thought to the mystical or implausible questions that go along with burning bushes or seas parting, even though the graphics clearly portrayed the water of the Red Sea standing completely vertical like a long corridor, much as it was depicted in *The Greatest Story Ever Told* and other early Hollywood movies. In spite of the cinematic marvels which were shown so graphically, I fear that it did much damage in encouraging a cult of literalism that has survived to become a wedge of unnecessary dimensions between faith, reason and science and then, even worse, ultimately spilling over into the realm of half-baked politics.

Years later, when I was myself a teenager, I became involved with the Anglican parish near my home and even became a Sunday School teacher in those days when that movement was at its height in the 1950s. I began to intuitively realize that there were ways of appreciating that things could be allegorical in nature. No one really needed to explain to me that when Jesus spoke of eating his flesh and drinking his blood it was obvious that this was meant in a mystical and spiritual way. Actually, one of the first times I began to take notice of things literal was when I was about eighteen and for some unknown reason, upon hearing in a sermon a reference to the phrase on Jesus' lips, "Take up your cross and follow me". I thought to myself, *Hang on a moment; this is happening long before the Crucifixion and Calvary—what is going on here?* However, I didn't let that sideline me for very long, as I was most certainly no biblical expert. But, one does entertain such questions, even if just in the course of thoughts that flash through the mind.

Fast forward now ten years and I find myself after a rather complex set of circumstances, in a classroom at the Anglican Theological College of British Columbia. It was one of the initial classes in Old Testament theology, and what better place to begin this adventure in theology than to be given the task of writing an essay on the authorship of the Pentateuch. The Anglican College, which unfortunately no longer exists, was in a collaborative relationship with Union College, of the United Church of Canada, where some of our classes were held jointly—mainly, Old Testament, Hebrew and Apologetics—and in this Old Testament class there were a number of Korean students belonging to the United Church who had come to Vancouver to pursue studies.

The various religious colleges were all in the same general location on the University of BC campus, and with regard to the Anglican and United Churches, which were at that time exploring the possibility of church union, all the Old Testament studies were done at Union College under the distinguished leadership of Dr. Vernon Fawcett, while the Greek and certain New Testament work was done at A.T.C. under the direction of Father Thomas Bailey.

During an infamous lecture on the subject of textual criticism and the authorship of the Pentateuch in preparation for the essays for that term there arose a ghastly row. The Koreans were horrified at the suggestion that anyone should dare to suggest that Moses might not have written all of it, but rather that it was a collection of the works of many authors and editors. It became rather a comic situation and I believe that part of the problem was because of the language difficulty, although, I think the theological significance was showing its soft underbelly quite visibly. This was probably one of the first overtly obvious times when I began to think of myself as being liberal—in theology and in other respects as well. The Koreans were so incensed—if that is an appropriate word to describe their behaviour—they were ready to pack their bags and return to Korea. Somehow, after much discussion and rational debate they managed to calm down and decided not to take such drastic action. There were many debates and heated discussions as we ploughed through our work in trying to understand the history of this very complex subject.

It was not until the mid-eighteen hundreds that the field of textual and historical criticism began in earnest in Germany. Of course scholars from the earliest centuries had expressed concerns about authorship and the method by which the scriptures have been transmitted. People like Irenaeus, Gregory of Nazianzus and St. Augustine of Hippo realized that the literature of the bible was not all to be taken literally. That is not to say they thought the ideas expressed were untrue but simply that in order to deal with such deep and philosophical concepts it was necessary to set them out in words that could be processed by ordinary people. It is rather akin to the use of the word *myth* in theological thinking. One hears reference to the *creation myth* for instance. Used in the theological sense this word is really a reference to a literary style. Unfortunately, the word has come down to us in modern English carrying the implication that something is 'false'. To begin talking about biblical criticism is also a red flag to many as the very word *criticism* has also taken on a pejorative implication. If you admit for a moment that something might have been copied inaccurately or that anything is questionable the fear seems to be that the whole house of cards will come tumbling down. This simply results in denial and the closing down of the thought processes completely.

We see this so often today as the debate about evolution and religion persists, even reaching out into the political sphere. It is not surprising why right wing religion and right wing politics co-exist so happily and why I sometimes want to tear my hair out while watching newscasts, especially at this time of looming political elections in both the U.S. and soon in Canada. I think it would not be untrue to say that this sort of reaction or *over*-reaction is in a large measure a North American phenomenon.

With religious people it is so often bound up with the notion that the bible is infallible, and of course, those who hold that position are quick to point out that it is the bible itself which claims to be infallible—a rather circular argument. It is that old self-proclaimed authority cycle. It is also why so often the extreme right readily falls into the trap of making the bible an idol to worship even as golden calves were in antiquity.

Looking over publications and articles about the Israelite Exile in Egypt during recent years I have become overwhelmed with the volume and diversity of related scholarship. There are times when I believe that over the past several years of retirement I have done more reading and research into theological issues than I actually did during my seminary years. The lines of thought and opinion are extremely diverse, from very detailed support to the historicity of the Exile noting place names and cultural knowledge of Egypt, down to those who do not believe that there ever was a massive Hebrew population there. It is obvious that some persons certainly had contact and knowledge of things Egyptian. History indicates that there was trade and interaction between Israelites and Egyptians and that there was a Jewish connection with communities in the north-west part of the Nile Delta. However, it seems that in Egyptian records there is almost nothing noted about these Israelites except for a scant few mentions about trade with Semitic people from the north, and curiously one of the items noted in an Egyptian list of trade items is a substance used, oddly enough, in the manufacture of eye-shadow of all things. This is set in the midst of a strong tradition of Egyptian record keeping and documentation.

Some articles and papers even suggest that an exile in Egypt never happened at all, but that perhaps during the Babylonian Exile the notion of a good story laden with such drama might encourage the unity of the Israelite nation and identity. It is perhaps one of those questions that we will never really understand. Tales of someone, presumably Joseph, being sold into bondage and countless other dramatic events have been common in Babylonian, Assyrian and other cultures.

An interesting aspect of my paper on the Pentateuch, which I mentioned had been a hand-in essay, was a comment to me written in the paper by my professor. It was beside that section where I wrote about the many plagues that struck Egypt during that period and the seasons of the year that they usually occurred. Incidentally, my professor had supplied a bibliography for use in the preparation of this essay, which included the book, <u>When Was the Pentateuch Written</u>? by G. Warrington, and was the source of much of my information about the historical period. The professor's note read:

"If such things were common in Egypt how do we explain the terror of the Egyptians and the recognition of the power of Israel's god in these events?"

Strangely, I do not recall having actually comprehended the intent of his remarks until now and, of course, I never did have occasion to speak with him personally about it. However, with hindsight, I think I might have responded, with as much diplomacy as I could muster, that after all the story *was* written by Hebrews and isn't their account of it much more melodramatic than if it had just been the expected events of the season? I'm sure he would have reminded me that these plagues were noted in the text to have been '*great*' and excessively severe rather than the normal yearly cycle of weather, insects and flooding.

These problems involve the theoretical and academic aspects of the biblical texts. However, there are other facets of the issue that impact upon the modern day involvement with biblical texts, especially with respect to their use in liturgy in the twenty-first century.

The Church, at least in those churches that have an understanding of liturgical continuity, is cognizant that a balanced and temperate use of scripture is important. Lectionaries of readings for public worship, rooted in the liturgical seasons and in compliance with the life of the community, are set out to be a guide and support for public and private worship. The danger in many non-liturgical churches is that the scriptural readings and meditations utilized are at the discretion of the worship leader. These, almost invariably, are the 'special interest' issues or hobbyhorses of the person called upon to expound them, which is remarkably counter productive and unbalanced.

During the years of my parish ministry there were countless times when I was asked to offer suggestions about the study of scripture or even asked if I could supply a copy of the bible for this use. So many times I was told that the person intended to 'read the bible from cover to cover'. This was surely said to impress me, but it didn't, and my response was always a suggestion that this would not be a very wise approach, in fact a rather precarious road to follow.

My suggestion was usually that they become involved with a reputable bible study group with a competent leader and to go methodically through perhaps first the Gospel of Mark and then onward to other New Testament writings. The other way of accomplishing this would be to get hold of a good, professional commentary on whatever was being studied and follow the reading with its assistance. One need not spend a lot of money doing this as libraries and colleges usually have plenty of such material. Not until there is some sort of undergirding in this kind of study should one ever dream of jumping into the most challenging and spiritually difficult issues in the Old Testament and especially the extremely mystical Revelation of St. John the Divine.

Over the course of the years I have spoken with so many people who tell me how well versed they are in the bible, even to the point of some claiming that they know all of the bible by the verse numbers. I never actually did it, but wished that I could have quizzed them on that to reveal how very mistaken they were. Of course, I suppose there are some people who have photographic memories for some odd reason, but I think for most people there are perhaps 40 or so texts that they do know by heart (their favourite issues naturally) but as to the rest of the bible they are really quite illiterate.

On one occasion at a clergy conference small groups of us were gathered for discussion. Someone raised the issue of our study of the bible and the important place the bible should have in the life of the parish. I could scarcely resist the temptation to be a little facetious and I said, "Well, I think the bible is highly overrated." That produced a rather sharp intake of breath around the table, but I think they did get my point and realized that I do take scripture seriously, although being aware of the pitfalls that can lurk there. In the context of that discussion I was able to recount the many times in my ministry that I had encountered groups that believed bible study should consist of someone reading a few verses and then everyone around the circle explaining what they thought it meant, completely without benefit of any training or knowledge.

There are other attitudes pertaining to the bible that are equally as exasperating. One evening some years ago I was walking down Granville Street in Vancouver on my way home from a meeting at about ten in the evening. I was wearing my clerical collar, which seems to have caught the attention of a young man who had been standing on a corner handing out pamphlets. He approached me, walked beside me since I did not stop, and was quite cordial and chatty. I was not certain which faith pattern he represented; he appeared to be a mainstream evangelical, perhaps Baptist or Pentecostal, although he was saying some things that sounded to be more representative of Jehovah's Witnesses, in spite of the fact that they are not generally so aggressive.

It was strangely consoling to think that just as I was unsure of his stance on things religious, he was surely misidentifying me—although whether I was Roman, Orthodox or Anglican would probably not have made any significant difference to him, I'm sure. I continued walking towards my car-park and he stayed right beside me, asking me probing questions as we went. He asked me if I believed in Jesus; if I believed in the Resurrection; did I believe in the bible; was I born again; was I saved, and so on. To all of these questions I was happily and honestly able to answer an unequivocal, "Yes". But, alas, this did not appear to satisfy him.

I asked him if he was saved and he naturally answered "Yes". I asked if he remembered just when that moment was and he noted a date, time and place which not surprisingly happened to be fairly recent. I purposefully asked that question in hopes that he would reciprocate and ask me the same thing, which he predictably did. He said, "And do you know when you were saved?" I replied that it happened at about three o'clock in the afternoon on that first Good Friday, just outside the walls of Jerusalem. It took him a few moments to digest that and I could almost see that the cogs in his head were spinning. In the brief silence that followed, I said in the most gentle tone I could manage, "You know, you are not the only Christian". The brief hesitation that followed all this chatter gave me at least the allusion that something profound and fundamental had actually penetrated him.

I will conclude this reflection on bible study and the essay on the Pentateuch specifically with an incident that happened to me years ago which underscores the truth of my assessment that generally, knowledge of the bible is very often pitifully weak.

While I was working in a parish near Edmonton, Alberta, Archdeacon Ed Thain, one of my clerical colleagues and my confessor, told me about a wonderful new commentary on the Pentateuch, with both the Hebrew and English texts, which had recently been published. It was by Rabbi Gunther Plaut of Holy Blossom Temple in Toronto. He and my friend had become involved in a number of projects over some years in the city of Toronto. Plaut's book was titled *The Torah,* which is a Hebrew word meaning *teaching* used to refer to the Pentateuch. So, off I went to see if the Canadian Bible Society store in Edmonton might have it. The Bible Society tends to cater to the evangelical end of the spectrum, but the Edmonton store was very large and did have a huge selection of material. I didn't know quite where to begin looking but after a time browsing in the Old Testament department and failing to find it I thought I should make an enquiry at the front desk. The young man I spoke to was very nattily dressed in a white shirt, tie and slacks as all young evangelical men seem to be. I imagined that he might be a high school student volunteering in the store on the weekend.

I was wearing my clerical collar at the time and when I mentioned to him that I was looking for a book called *The Torah* by Rabbi Plaut, he drew himself up to his full imperious height and said in a rather sarcastic way, "Sir, this is a Christian bookstore!" I simply let that go, took an order form to fill in, and they eventually acquired a copy for me.

Incidentally, while I am thinking in terms of just what evangelism is, it was about this same time period that a very prominent American evangelist held a crusade in Edmonton, Alberta. It was apparently heavily attended in a local stadium. About two weeks after the crusade I received three letters from the association that had put on the event. The letters separately named three women from my parish and in each case indicated that they were *troubled* or words to that effect. The three were specifically mentioned in the letters and had each obviously been interviewed about their status, hence our parish and my name were noted. The phraseology of each letter was almost identical. At first I was somewhat perplexed and wondered what was going on. Had I been remiss in not detecting problems? I made a point of visiting these three women within a week in my cycle of parish visitation, even though I saw all of them weekly at church, as my curiosity was piqued.

During my visits with them I did not mention anything about the letters or the Crusade and in each case in the course of our chatting they volunteered having attended the event as it was a once in a lifetime opportunity and they were interested in experiencing it. It is quite possible that the three had attended the Crusade together. They all mentioned that they had gone forward at the 'altar call' since they were involved and committed Christians. I was relieved to see that none of them appeared to have any particular spiritual issues and needless to say, I did not mention the letters but it is rather telling how many people who conduct this kind of evangelism approach it making definite and unfounded assumptions about others. I looked into the procedures of the Crusade to learn more about how the event is organized. I discovered that counsellors are chosen from local congregations and that many of them are teenagers who, I'm sure, must be new Christians who are in that space where they are very hot for Jesus and understand all the answers to the complex questions of faith.

TWO

THE DOCTRINE OF MAN
Old Testament III
January 12, 1967

For the Church and the Bible, the apex of God's creation was Mankind. In the Old Testament we find many references to the place which man is to occupy within God's scheme of Creation. Man has certain responsibilities to both God and his fellow man and throughout the scriptures we see this idea set forth and developed.

In order to set out on an attempt to show the relationship between man and his place in the natural order I will begin with a quote from Karl Barth. He says, "The covenant is the goal of creation, creation is the way to the covenant". This at least indicates that there is a very close tie between man's responsibility to God and his place within God's plan. The structure within bounds of which man acts is supplied by God yet man is given freedom—

he is autonomous. This autonomous nature of both God and man is necessary in order that a covenant relationship might be established. Man is able to choose according to his own will whether or not he wants to obey and acknowledge God.

Within this natural order man has a certain amount of confidence concerning the world in which he lives. He has God's promise that the world will continue on its course without mishap as we see in the covenant which was made after the flood (Gen. 8:22) "While the earth remains, seed time and harvest, cold and heat, summer and winter, day and night, shall not cease." God's providence and His concern for men can be seen also in terms of the natural order. On certain occasions God was known to interrupt the natural functioning of the world in order to protect His chosen people. Examples of this are the crossing of the Red Sea and the fording of the Jordan River in order to allow the Hebrews to enter the Promised Land. Creation was part of God's plan, which eventually led to the covenant and to the expressing of His love for the whole of humanity through Israel.

THE HEBREW CONCEPTION OF CREATION

The Israelites had a view of creation and of their role in the created order, which was distinctive amongst ancient peoples. For the Hebrew People the creation myth was closely bound up with history. This was not so with most other theories of creation. In the Babylonian world the myth of Marduk and Tiamat was never tied to real history. Stories involving such mythical creatures as Rehab and Leviathan are nevertheless put into the context of history. There is more the feeling of historical background than of simply a mythological background in the Hebrew Creation drama. God personally takes part in every act of creation. He opens the mother's womb, Gen. 4:1, 25, 18:10, He gives the animals their food, Psalm 145:15, and He gives light each day, Amos 5:8.

Man is intended to be a master of God's creation and to subdue it. When man, through sin, falls he even drags creation down with him. The trees of paradise are replaced by thorns and thistles and the soil thereafter only produces at great expense of effort. In The Theology of the Old Testament, Edmond Jacob says that: "sin involves the danger of undermining the integrity of creation and a return to chaos." (p. 141)

The Garden of Eden was planted, for man—for his own needs and pleasures. Before God brought Eden into being the world was a desert waste. Man was to be the tender and gardener in his new domain and was intended by God to have dominion over the creatures of the earth. It would be true to say that the material universe was brought into being for the express purpose of being a stage on which the human drama could be acted out.

It is interesting to note that there was really no essential difference between man and the other animals that inhabited the world. They were both made from the same "dust" of the earth and in the same way. At the time of the flood men as well as animals were condemned and the same promises were made for each. In the end they both come to share in the same fate—death. However, man was associated with God in a special way. He was not a semi-divine creature as we see in certain other cultures, but he was placed in an independent and autonomous situation where he had rationality and responsibility and because of this he is allied to God.

In one of the accounts of creation (Gen. 2:4b) God creates man first and then the animals. This account is regarded by many people as being the most ancient one. In Genesis 8:19 man gives the animals their names, by doing so he has power over them, and creation is subject to man.

One of the rather interesting problems of the Creation story is the one revolving around the idea that man was created in God's image. All of the references to this are found in the Book of Genesis, and at that, in the Priestly Code. There are several words used in this connection. The word 'tselem' means image and it implies concreteness and outward appearance. Another word 'demut', which is used to translate likeness, implies something not quite so material. Some scholars have attempted to show that the writer meant to differentiate between two kinds of likeness but this is improbable. The two words are more likely simply to be complementing one another in the typical Hebrew poetic style.

Often in ancient times a king would erect statues of himself in far corners of his empire where it was very difficult to visit personally. In this way he could in a sense be present. Thus the idea of presence came to be attached to images.

Some have suggested that the thing that separates man from the animals is his upright walking position. Such ideas would certainly seem to indicate that some people believed that men resembled God in outward appearance, and this is possibly why animals rather than men were chosen to represent evil in Biblical writing. In the Garden we have the serpent, which represented Satan, and in Daniel beasts symbolize the forces of darkness. Man seems to have been God's representative. Man is meant to maintain his relationship with the Father, when for some reason he attempts to jump out of his role (as in the Garden of Eden when Adam and Eve were tempted to be like God) then man falls to the animal level. Man is God's vice regent on earth and he must fulfil his function.

ANTHROPOMORPHISM
IN THE OLD TESTAMENT

Even though the Hebrews saw mankind as being created in the image of God they did not always conceive of Him as being in human form. He is often depicted in fire, clouds and in many other supernatural phenomena. But there are the instances where He is seen as a man or rather, in human form (Is. 4, Ezek 1, and Daniel 7). But again, in Hosea 11:9 and in Isaiah 51:3 it is stressed that God is not a man and in Exodus 35:18, 34:29 and in Isaiah 6:2 God is claimed to be invisible. The Bible, however, does not attempt to make a doctrine of God either in physical images or in images of the mind; in fact the whole question of the being of God is pretty much avoided. Man is made in the image of God in that he has the capacity to love, to reason and to exercise his will.

MAN AND WOMAN

In the creation narrative we see God creating woman from man and the fulfilment of their being is in the union of marriage as one flesh. Woman is, nevertheless, seen as subordinate to man. Man by himself is a complete being and woman adds nothing to his nature. Woman owes her existence to man. The place of woman is in the home—as a helpmate to her husband. Genesis 2:23 points out the close affinity between man and woman: "This at last is bone of my bones, and flesh of my flesh; she shall be called woman, because she was taken out of man." Fertility is seen as a blessing from God and children are the sign of His grace. Man and woman are seen to be on equal footing as far as sexual differences are concerned. A monogamous relationship is the normal situation and it is implied in Genesis 2 that bigamy is wrong. It is also part of Hebrew thinking on this subject that woman's dependence on man is the result of sin. Pregnancy and childbirth are the signs of this. Woman belongs to her husband's household and is his possession.

SIN – BROKEN RELATIONSHIP

There is really no systematic doctrine of sin in the Old Testament. The word chet, חטא (which means 'to miss') is wrongness or a revolt against God. There is no actual word for sin in Hebrew. Missing the mark was the phrase meaning the same as the concept of sinning. A teaching like the Christian doctrine of original sin did not exist. Sin was disobedience to God and the breaking of the relationship with Him. The Law was the method by which God exercised His sovereign will over His people and the breaking of the Law (the Commandments) was an act of sin and a breach of this relationship.

This Important relationship was not just one between the individual and God—it was really one between God, the community and the particular man. Every man was a representative of the community. When Achan sinned against God by keeping some of the enemy treasure, which was forbidden by the law, he caused a rift between the whole community and God. Eventually Achan along with his whole family was completely wiped out. His sin was not a private affair. Every person in the community is called to be a responsible individual.

MAN AS A LIVING BEING

There are a number of concepts, which are valuable in explaining just how man has his being and how he interacts in the physical world and in the realm of the spirit. First we will examine those ideas, which have to do with man's very life.

The term nephesh, נפש (which has a very wide range of meaning) is what man received when God breathed into his nostrils the breath of life. This was not given in the sense of a soul that is placed somewhere in the body, but it is the result of divine activity—it is at the same time physical and spiritual. This is what makes man an individual. 'Nephesh chayyah' is a term that implies a living being in its external aspects. It can mean both breath and blood. At death it is the breath which ceases and thus the idea that this is the seat of life. Or sometimes it is the blood, which is poured out, and thus the same connection with blood.

Flesh בשר (basar)

This word 'basar' in the beginning meant an outward appearance but ended up as a word denoting the whole man. Basar is connected with skin, rather than to bones. Man has this in common with other living beings. It came to mean the entire body. This concept can be associated with the seat of the spiritual faculties as well as of fleshly desires. Flesh is what distinguished man from God but it would be unreasonable to conclude that there was in any sense a spirit-matter dualism. It is rather a contrast between strength and weakness.

Spirit: רוּחַ (ruach)

The spirit, or ruach, is something that Yahweh possesses in its fullness—the power that creates life. Without the spirit there is no life. In some instances it is portrayed as having a certain quality of violence, which enables men to perform extraordinary tasks. Sometimes when the spirit leaves a man he is dissipated, lacking much of his former vitality. He is not really a whole nephesh.

Heart: לֵב (lev)

The word lev means middle. This is possibly why the heart (which is in the middle of the body) was thought to be the centre of life. It is contrasted with the face —as Jonah went into the heart of the deep as opposed to the face of the deep. The heart is the soul in its inner value. The Hebrews were astute enough to notice that impressions from outside could affect the heart, either accelerating it or retarding it.

It was the source of life, and the seat of religious knowledge. God alone fortifies and establishes the hearts of men and the heart belongs to God alone.

OBLIGATION TO FAMILY AND STATE

In the Hebrew world children were from the earliest age trained to value and respect the community. Boys were taken under the wings of their fathers and schooled in manners, religion, the father's trade and many other things while girls were trained by their mothers. Boys moved out into much wider circles than the girls did and there was a great emphasis put on the change that marked his entrance into public life. The place of women in the community was as attentive wives and also they spent considerable time looking after the poor and other charitable concerns. The son learned wisdom from his father and was trained in personal relationships, in religion and in observances and customs. Tradition was passed on in living form.

Women were always under the guardianship of men. First their fathers were responsible and then their husbands. If a woman's husband should die, she then came under his brother's or his father's guardianship. The most disastrous plight of a woman was to have no protector. Naomi, whose name was Mara (bitter) was one such woman. As maturity came quite early to Hebrew young people, so did responsibility.

The relationship of the individual person was tied to the larger life of the community by four spheres or aspects of life. First there was the realm of religious practice, which was the responsibility of every true Israelite. The other areas were marriage, Law and warfare. The community as a whole was closely related to the sacrifices, even though the Priestly narratives would tend to obscure this. David and his army were purified by Ahimelech before they could eat of the holy bread at Nob indicating that the whole body of them had to be in a correct relationship with God. Marriage was the command of God; "Be ye fruitful and multiply."

The family was the smallest yet the most important social unit of the community. It was the most natural community. The idea of a bachelor in the Hebrew community was quite unheard of— in fact Hebrew does not even have a word for this concept. Law played an extremely important part in the lives of Yahweh's people. Not only did they live in very close contact with one another but they were continually passing judgement upon one another—regarding behaviour and attitudes. Hebrew children simply grew up in this ethos. They were trained to ask about law and to become proficient in the eloquent dialogues concerning it. This was really a great body of tradition and custom giving a pattern to the thought of the whole community concerning what is right in certain situations—attempting to bring true justice to the individual as a member of the community. It was the responsibility of the whole assembly of men, who would gather at the 'gate' to puzzle over and decide each case. Younger men listened to the older men and sat outside the 'circle'. Eventually, when they became responsible they were admitted to the group.

Protecting the rights of the community was a continual battle for the Hebrew people. They had to be constantly wary of animals of prey, which threatened their flocks as well as of thieves and other human enemies. The males of the community were of necessity trained in the use of weapons.

The concept of the importance of the group before the individual has been branded 'corporate personality'. The clan and the nation were paramount. This is manifested in the idea of blood revenge which said that if a man of one particular group was treated unjustly by another group, someone from that other group must suffer in order to effect satisfaction. This is the same principle that lies behind the family feud. If a man sins against the community often his whole family, along with his flocks and possessions, would be annihilated. The same principle lies behind the custom of a brother taking his brother's place in marriage if he were to die. This principle is also seen in the willingness of Abraham to offer the life of his son Isaac and in the offering of Jephtha's daughter.

The word sod, סוֹד, means a council—the body of men of the community who sit together and decide each individual case set before them. The word implies the idea of a circle and undoubtedly comes from the positions that the men took while deliberating. They acted upon each other's will and eventually arrive at a decision, or became of one heart. There was no compulsion to attend this assembly, but it was considered the duty of each man to take his part in the sod. Each evening they would discuss the news of the day and plan projects that concerned the whole community.

THE DIVINE STRUCTURE OF THE COMMUNITY

Throughout the whole life of the community one can detect the pervasive presence and influence of Yahweh. The very actions, attitudes and thoughts of the Hebrew people were closely associated with the life and action of God Himself.

The word 'berakhah' ברכה or 'blessing' is associated with happiness. The man who is happy is blessed. Offspring, riches, possessions and victory over enemies are all signs of blessing. E. Jacob in his book, The Theology of the Old Testament, says that blessing is "the power by which life is maintained and augmented".

The idea of covenant love, 'chesed' (חסד), although it seems to have no equivalent in either Greek or English, seems to mean 'divine fidelity'. In translating the scriptures from Hebrew to Greek, the Septuagint translators used the Greek word ελεος (eleos) to substitute for chesed but in a number of cases they used the word that denotes strength. The word ελεος would usually be translated 'mercy' in English.

> "All flesh is as grass and all its strength as the flower of the field." (Isaiah 40:6)

Yahweh is חסד, 'chesed'—a fortress or a shield. Chesed is also a bond uniting God and man, and man to God, in a loyal relationship. God's chesed, or loyalty, is revealed through the covenant.

The term צדיק, tsedek, or 'righteousness' denotes that which is right, stable and substantial. A thing is tsedek when it conforms to the norm of what it should be. We have examples of the word being used in connection with right balances and just weights. It is a concept of relationship fashioned on everyday dealings. Rather than being a state of affairs, it is action. A man is righteous because he acts justly, he does not act justly because he is righteous. The Old Testament speaks of God's righteousness when it is manifest in His behaviour in history. Peace, or shalom, is the result of blessing, which is experienced in times of abundance and prosperity. It can only be fully attained in the last times but for the righteous it can certainly be a present reality.

TRANSLATIONS OF HEBREW TO GREEK

One of the problems that have cropped up as a result of the translation of the Hebrew Bible into Greek is the maintaining of the Hebrew concepts in the new language. For years people have read into the scriptures the concepts of Greek thought rather than of the Hebrew because of the use of the Greek words. It has to be remembered that the background of the Hebrew religion is rooted in Moses, the Law and the Prophets rather than in Plato and the other Greek philosophers. Concepts and ideas of the Old Testament have been carried on into the New Testament.

The New Testament cannot be read as a body of Greek literature in spite of the fact that the language is Greek. Another commonly held attitude, which led to complication, was that the Greek of the New Testament could be compared with the Greek of the classical period. New Testament Greek in this light was found to be wanting. Therefore in any study of the New Testament texts, it must be remembered that the roots were Hebrew and that a close examination of the way in which the Hebrew concepts were rendered in the Greek Septuagint is mandatory. Usually there is no problem in the translations from Hebrew to Greek as far as meaning is concerned but it seems that in those few places where confusion enters in, is where the most important and distinctive ideas of the Old Testament are represented. Paul seems to use language that encompasses both Hebrew and Greek concepts. His use of the idea of 'teaching' has a Hebrew background, while the idea of 'principle' has a distinctive Greek background. He deals at great length with the concept of the 'Law' which has its roots in both languages. James seems to be oriented very much in the Greek tradition, as is evidenced in his dissertation on 'faith' and 'law', (James 2:17).

Hellenistic scholars like Clement of Alexandria and Origen far too often read the New Testament as a Greek book and this leads to problems innumerable. This of course is the fate of the Bible into whichever language it is translated. The Reformation, as some people believe, was the point at which there was a distinctive break with the Greek oriented tradition.

A few of the most important ideas, which are often seen in the wrong light because of a lack of understanding, are noted below:

Righteousness (δικαιοσυνη):

This word has the same meaning as the Hebrew tsedek, which means conforming to a norm. The view of St. John Chrysostom and many others, which was 'to make righteous', held sway for quite a number of years. The second, and more realistic interpretation is 'to declare righteous'. There have been many arguments about which way this should be translated. Paul, in Romans 4:5, speaks of δικαιουν, the 'ungodly', which in Hellenistic Greek could be translated "to condemn the ungodly". It must always be remembered that the LXX (Septuagint) always seems to use language in a favourable way and therefore it is unlikely that this is a valid translation. If the word is to be translated 'to declare righteous', then why would God declare a sinner righteous if he was not? Could it be because righteousness was a necessary condition of salvation? It would seem not! Paul fought this idea all through his writing. He repeatedly drives home the idea that all that is required by God is faith

and repentance. In the Greek language
δικαιουν has a juridical or even a forensic
connotation and the word has probably
been translated with this in mind far too
often. The Hebrew sense has far less of this
implication than was previously expected.
There is a sense of judgment connected
with it certainly, but more in the worldwide
sense than that of the courtroom. It was
intimately bound up with the affairs of men.
In Paul's writing there is the double usage
but it would be safe to say that he uses it in
the fullest sense of salvation—ethical
righteousness! In other words it is God
who makes possible righteousness. In
Romans 4:3, the story of Abraham's
intended offering of his son Isaac the
actions of Abraham are not ethically sound
but the whole point is that he is forgiven on
the basis of faith. Paul does not condone
the act itself but he acknowledges that this
is an act of faith. Because Abraham came
to God in faith he was counted righteous.
Thus the order of priority seems to be
firstly faith, then salvation, and then
righteousness.

Covenant-Love (chesed):

This word 'chesed' is the one, which in the Hebrew carried the meaning of mercy, loving-kindness and pity. Sometimes this was translated into the Greek language by the word ελεος which was 'pity for man's misery. For this idea of God's covenant-love for those whom He had chosen Paul uses the word χαρις or grace. This is the free gift of God—given of God's love and undeserved on man's part. Paul seems to use χαρις and αγαπη interchangeably. The love that God continually manifests toward mankind is a completely free gift.

Spirit (ruach):

The Greek word πνευμα is used in all of the same ways that the Hebrew word 'ruach' is used. It means, in each language, breath, wind or spirit. It is the breath of life —the vital principle of man, as opposed to the word σαρξ, 'flesh'. It is used for corporeal spirits of every type—both of angels and evil spirits. Sometimes it is represented as being quite violent. In Luke 9:39 we read,

> "and behold, a spirit seizes him, and he suddenly cries out;

> it convulses him till he foams,
> and shatters him, and will
> hardly leave him."

This is a typical reference to an evil spirit and we have already noted that in the Hebrew the word can have the same usage.

The concept of 'Ruach-adonai' or in the Greek, πνευμα κυριου, the Spirit of the Lord is the life creating spirit.

In the New Testament we are brought face to face with the fact that there was a vast difference between the Hebrew and the Greek attitudes toward life. Hebrew thought was oriented around the 'Knowledge of God' while Greek thought was interested in man's higher nature —'Know Thyself'. The Greek attitudes are really found nowhere in the Bible—only the Hebrew thought can be detected. Many of the problems that biblical interpretation has faced have been because the Bible has far too often been translated and interpreted with a Greek mindset rather than in a Hebrew way.

Fr. Donald Andrew Dodman

REFLECTIONS ON THE DOCTRINE OF MAN
March 2012

In the long term scheme of things 45 years is a relatively short period of time, however in my mind's eye I can see just how far mankind has progressed, at least in certain respects. I did not write the original essay believing in a literalistic way the ideas that were a part of that 3,000 year old world-view. My perspective was more historical and rooted in the fact that I was writing about the literature, texts and theological mythology in which it was presented as well as endeavouring to evaluate it in a scholarly way. It is appalling, nevertheless, how some of those attitudes still remain with us in our twenty-first century world.

For a little diversion, and perhaps to spark my imagination as I contemplated how to approach this diverse subject, I opened YouTube on my computer to see if I might find some inspiration and perspective—a springboard, if you will. I found some clips that dealt with the question of creation and soon found a very interesting one called "Journey to the end of the Universe" which gives a compressed overview of the universe including some of the most up to date scientific assessments and theories about origins and size. Much of it was far beyond the comprehension of a nonscientific mind, although it was thoroughly fascinating. Contemplating the immensity of the universe is indeed mind blowing. The clip was perhaps 6 minutes long and for those interested it might be worth Googling to find it. I will not include a link here because there are dozens of similar clips, which deal with the size, and nature of the universe and they are mostly all worth exploring if one has the inclination.

As I watched the animated recreation of the Big Bang and the expanding universe I was humbled just as I had been as a teenager looking into the night sky at sea knowing that the stars I was seeing were many, many light years distant. I did not realize at the time that all the stars that are visible to the naked eye are within the Milky Way, our own galaxy, nor did I realize that beyond what I could see—far beyond—there were untold numbers of other such galaxies. I learned not too long ago that there actually is one object not in our

Milky Way Galaxy which we can faintly see with the naked eye, and that is the Andromeda Galaxy, (in the constellation Andromeda) which appears to resemble a faint and fuzzy star. It is, of course, 2.5 million light years away and is larger than the Milky Way. I speak of the Big Bang with a slight nod toward the mythical because the theory, as popularly explained, is perhaps even more fantastic than the literal biblical explanation of Creation. But, nevertheless, here it is and we are a part of it.

The narrator spoke of how modern science and technology, with the aid of such things as the Hubble telescope and other calculations and tests, had determined that the known size of the universe was in the hundreds of billions of light years across. The graphics and photographs made it all seem so utterly immense, which indeed, it is. It was well noted that what we can comprehend is undoubtedly only a tiny scratch on the surface.

The world-view of the writers of the Hebrew scriptures was just that—a scratch on the surface of the nature of mankind. For all intents and purposes I understood it to be an affirmation of the dignity of human kind. At the time of writing I believe I had somewhat of a more developed idea of the universe but time certainly has shown that much can change in a half century. When I was writing in 1967 not very much about the subject concerned me to any degree. It was an adventure to be delving into scripture and the *science* of theology and to be learning about the relatively recent approaches to analyzing scripture from the historical and literary perspective. However, at that time the deeper and more important elements of what the scriptures were saying did not really have a significant impact upon me.

Looking back at the essay of 45 years ago, I pondered about how far we have come in one sense. At the time of writing that essay my awareness was so very limited. It would not be until the year after I graduated and was ordained that the first manned moon landing occurred in 1969. Similarly, when I went to sea as a teenager with the Canadian Navy, there was no such thing as global positioning satellites. Navigation was still a very fundamental procedure—star, sextant and chronometer as well as good doses of guessing and dead reckoning when the sky was overcast.

As I read the essay again, all these years later, I am appalled when I realize what the

Hebrews were actually saying about the nature of mankind. It was not surprising that the Hebrews believed that humankind was the crowning achievement of God and that the things of the earth—the fertile land and the plants and animals—were for the use of man. I understood that much of what the Old Testament spoke about was allegorical and was gleaned from what the writers had experienced in their lives millennia ago. They were rooted in a tribal society, which was doing its best to fend off outsiders and make a niche for themselves in that tiny corner of the world at the eastern end of the Mediterranean Sea.

Considering the brutal world in which they lived and some of the activities and customs of many of their neighbours, the Hebrews were actually making some remarkable advances. They were totally convinced that there was only one Creator who had made all things, and they devised some valuable insights into the moral realms of righteousness and fairness. They were instinctively aware that in order for the world to work properly there had to be law, justice and a respect for one another. The idea that all things, especially physical matter, are understood to be good and of the Creator's design was a breakthrough and was revolutionary at that time.

It was also visionary in declaring that there could only be one God amongst many local gods, and that man was invited to come into a covenant relationship with God, which led inevitably to the concept of sin and righteousness in human life.

The Nation of Israel was definitely on the right track in its stress on the importance of community. When adversity struck or when the people needed to make decisions it was so important for them to *meet at the gate* to talk and come to some sort of consensus. The very notion of deliberating together for this purpose was a novel and creative exercise.

My paper on the Doctrine of Man was, of course, intended to encompass the Old Testament view of this particular aspect of relationship to the Almighty since it was within the scope of Old Testament studies. To include later Hebrew developments or progress within the life of the Christian Church would, of course, have been impossible to cope with in one essay. However, for a balanced and fair treatment of the subject here, I feel that there is a whole dimension that needs to be addressed otherwise any discerning reader would surely feel that this effort would remain only half answered.

During my years of ministry I worked for some time with Aboriginal Peoples for whom a sense of community was of great importance. They had independently, in the mists of time, come to the realization that when people of such small and close knit communities needed to make decisions they had to sit down together to talk and debate. This was particularly important in the coastal villages of British Columbia, where isolation was often a major fact of life. People lived closely together on the islands or in the valleys reaching down to the sea in this mountainous country. It was very like the camps in the north and the central plains where people depended upon one another for the ordering of their communities with regard to defence and the provision of food. I always sensed that their way of dealing with community issues was ingenious, albeit slow. There would be much talk, *at the gate* and usually it took a great deal of time before consensus was reached. The value of it, however, was that this process avoided the situation where some might go away from the meeting feeling elated that they had won or depressed and angry to have lost the argument.

I believe that many of our problems in western society are magnified because of our political systems where votes are taken and where there are definitely winners and losers. People become aligned with particular views and this leads swiftly to division and intolerance. We see this played out, especially in North America, every time there is an election cycle. The bad feeling and hatred seems to compound and grow so that the system itself becomes the reason for existing, leaving the wellbeing of the individual constituents almost out of the equation. At the time of writing we happen to be in an election cycle, both in the United States and just a few years off in Canada, and it is often frustrating and wearisome to see the process painfully working its way out day after day.

One of the aspects of the original essay, which I found to be the cause of some present measure of dismay, is the issue of Man's—and I definitely mean "male" here—superiority . Woman is created to be a helpmate and a companion for man but is very obviously considered to be an inferior being. She is the possession of men just like any other property. Unfortunately, this view has not really vanished from human life even though considerable advance has been made. There seems to be a segment of our society, which dwells upon such issues and sadly sometimes attempts to justify the view by using these very ancient texts as a template. Reason, in so much of the debate, seems to take the backseat. This seems to be the case not only in church thinking but also in large parts of secular society. It is not surprising that fundamentalist, flat-earth religious thinking finds itself in good company with legalism of all stripes. This is one of the negative aspects of the Hebrew devotion to the Law.

I suppose that if one takes any asset and elevates it out of all proportion it can inevitably turn sour and lead to a host of other problems. Following on the accounts of creation and man's entry onto the scene eventually one comes face to face with the book of Leviticus which is an exposition of the Law in what I should think is extreme detail. Here, in the Holiness Code, one finds exact details, which govern what one can wear and eat as well as what one can or cannot do at particular times. It has been said before that no one could possibly observe all of these restrictions and remain sane. Many of the Laws found there are accompanied by declarations of anathema—that it is an abomination, for which one could be stoned to death. A few examples of such anathemas are divorcing and remarrying, adultery, cursing parents, breaking the Sabbath, and for a woman to be found not to be a virgin on her wedding night.

To attempt to address or analyze the vast problem that this opens would, of course, require another book or perhaps more. However, I will attempt to provide a few examples of how the matter has played out over time.

It did not take very long after the Resurrection and the foundation of the church for difficulties to begin to emerge. One of the first controversies is even recorded in the Book of the Acts of the Apostles. It involved the rite of circumcision. A council was called by James, Bishop of the Jerusalem Church and took place in about 50 AD. Paul was summoned to this Council because it was known that he did not believe that circumcision was necessary for his gentile converts. This particular incident was perhaps the first time that anyone actually acknowledged that there was any difference between Christianity and Judaism. The incident in question is recorded in Acts 15 and it sounds as though there was quite a furore stirred up between the Jerusalem Church and Paul. It seems that there was a vigorous and long discussion about it. I will have considerably more to say about Paul in a subsequent essay.

Throughout the ages the Christian Community has had to wrestle with Old Testament texts since the Church was seen as a continuation of its Jewish antecedents. This meant that there had to be a compromise regarding just how much of the Hebrew text was to be binding on Christians. I suppose that there had always been a struggle to understand which customs were vital to the faith and which were to be considered allegorical. Even within Judaism today that struggle continues. Which foods are actually forbidden and how one might cope with celebrating the Sabbath in modern times. It would without a doubt be virtually impossible to live observing every word and demand of the bible. Some claim that they can and do live that way but I highly doubt it. There always seems to be a way around those perturbing texts.

When I think about this situation an amusing scene springs to my mind. It was in the movie "Lawrence of Arabia". Peter O'Toole as Lawrence is invited into the tent of King Faisal to talk. The King pours wine for the two of them. He dips his finger into his glass and shakes off a drop of wine onto the ground. After a toast and the first sip of wine Lawrence says, *"But I thought you were not supposed to drink alcohol"*. The King responds,

"Well, Orence, the Holy Koran says, 'Thou shalt not drink one drop of wine'."

The texts of the Torah have always been subject to interpretation. In Jesus' time there were often clashes about such things and the Gospels are full of references to the clashes between the Pharisees, Sadducees and the Scribes. The Sadducees were very conservative and rigid about scripture, regarding it as the only authority given by God, while the Pharisees gave oral tradition equal weight. The present debate about scripture and authority are by no means anything new.

Unfortunately, in the past few decades many church people have reverted to what they consider to be a literalistic interpretation of scripture, especially when that seems to support and strengthen their preferred ideas. I am reminded of a story that was told by the principal of my theological college during a liturgy class dealing with the sacrament of baptism. As a young priest he had worked with Cree people in Manitoba. On one occasion, while he was preparing a number of families for the baptism of their children, he indicated that they should consult the Bible in selecting baptismal names for their children. On the day of the baptisms, one of the sets of parents stepped forward to the font with their infant son and in the course of the baptismal liturgy were asked to "Name this child". Having taken Fr. Blewett's advice seriously and having duly consulted the Bible, they announced, "His name is Barabbas". In the urgency of the moment and with a church full of people, instead of trying to explain things or to make an issue of it, Father simply took the child, poured water from the font and said, "Barnabas, I baptize thee in the Name of the Father and of the Son and of the Holy Ghost. Amen".

With regard to the question of interpretation of scripture in the life of the Church today, it is quite amazing how Anglicans (where my roots were nourished) have managed to keep peace and unity for almost five centuries given that there have always been varying interpretations and practices. For most of its history the English Church has tolerated churchmanship preferences and managed to remain reasonably unified with a few difficult times during the catholic revival of the mid-18 hundreds. Catholic and protestant views have lived side by side with a minimum of disunity. The Methodist movement was perhaps the most obvious display of fracture that the Church of England encountered. The Anglo-

Catholic movement even remained *in communion* to the present day. However, at this time things seem to be going off the rails with alarming speed. Groups within the Anglican Communion are splitting off with regularity, often because some are lured back to a legalistic interpretation of the letter of the law, and frequently because they seem to be attracted to a pietistic, self-righteous style of Christianity. This is often found to be the case when embracing a literalistic view of the bible. It is particularly true with regard to views of sexuality, which for some odd reason appears now to be the topic *du jour* in many church and even secular circles like an obsession. Pitifully, the age of enlightenment has not yet dawned in some quarters.

Before proceeding with thoughts and examples concerning church order and discipline I should clarify how Anglicans—at least in Canada and many other parts of the world—decide about matters of practice. The church is divided up into dioceses, which are led by bishops and are basically autonomous. On a yearly basis in most dioceses the bishop and clergy together with representative lay people from the various parishes meet in a synod during which matters of financial, social and pastoral concerns are discussed and put into practice. It is almost like any other secular political gathering and is basically democratic in nature, except that the Anglican Church is episcopally led—that is by a bishop, and so when certain matters of discussion are voted upon it is done by houses; the house of the laity; the house of clergy and the house of bishops. In some large dioceses there may be an assistant bishop or bishops. On most housekeeping issues such as finances and buildings the synodical body votes together and a simple majority decides the outcome with the bishop giving his or her approval but who can, in certain circumstances, withhold that approval. (This question will arise again later on in this volume.) For certain vital issues the three houses will vote separately and a predetermined proportion of each house must be achieved. For instance for the election of a bishop it might happen that there is required a two thirds majority in the houses of the clergy and laity so that a definite portion of the synod is in agreement, and then the Bishop either approves or withholds approval.

During the past sixty or so years many bodies within the Anglican Communion have made modest advances in teaching and discipline, for instance, with regard to remarriage after a divorce and on the question of the use of contraception. I recall as a child that a divorced friend of the family who was Anglican was definitely unwelcome at the altar rail to receive communion. Remarriage in the church was frankly out of the question. Eventually that changed as the church began to wrestle with the issue and to realize that the subtleties and nuances of married life impacted heavily upon married partners. Also, the church was beginning to grasp that there were situations where some marriages were simply beyond the point of no return, where no good intentions or counselling was ever going to be able to salvage them.

Now, here we are at the beginning of the twenty-first Century when a new controversy concerning marriage rises to the surface. That is the question of same-sex partnerships. Up until the current debates about it, most people have simply realized that those kinds of associations exist and probably always have, but were content to let it be and just avoid talking about it. But now, for a multitude of reasons including the need to be up-front and honest and not letting same-sex relationships be relegated to the closet, as well as issues of inheritance and insurance and other benefits that most other people take for granted, people are raising questions about human rights and dignity. Why should I be embarrassed or ashamed of this wonderful person who shares my life and who gives it quality and meaning?

I referred to such relationships a moment ago as 'partnerships' possibly because it was the terminology I was used to years ago, but that does smack of avoiding actually approaching the real issue—the elephant in the room. What gay people want and expect is to be treated equally as anyone else would. Back in 2003, my partner Devan and I were going through the process of sorting out the complexities of immigration for him as he is American. In the midst of all that, British Columbia passed a bill allowing for same-sex marriage, which was full marriage with all the implications. That changed the whole nature of the immigration process and things were sorted out very quickly. The process began with a province here and a province there, but it quickly became the law for the whole of Canada. We are both entirely grateful for the progressive attitudes of Canada.

Now this issue is becoming a topic of great debate in the U.S. and states are gradually dealing with it, but it seems to be a slow process. We laugh as we watch the news items about it on TV where one repeatedly hears politicians saying, "It will destroy heterosexual marriage" or "God will send disaster on America if this happens". And then there are those who repeat *ad nauseam* 'marriage is between a man and a woman' as though this is a Biblical quote, which it is not. It is actually laughable to listen to it. Most if not all gay people were born to heterosexual parents for starters, and secondly even those marriages are in crisis as about 50% of all marriages in the US and Canada end in divorce anyway. It is amusing to hear the mantra repeated about 'one man and one woman' because the actual teaching of the Bible varies from one man and six hundred women to 'marriage is between one man and one woman, FOREVER', with little or no possibility of a second, or third go at it.

This relationship with others, to which Jesus beckons us, is seen in a profound way in a prayer written by Abbé Michel Quoist. The 'secret' of the delinquent is not actually articulated, but I find that personally I think I understand it and have indeed worn the shoes of both the boy and the priest. The prayer is surely an outline of what prayer can and should be—the very essence of what Man is called to be.

THE DELINQUENT

I know his secret,
His weighty secret.

How, Lord, can it be carried by this big boy with the childish face grown old too soon?

I wanted him to tell it to me,
To give it to me to bear with him.
For long months now I have been stretching my hand
    towards this young, crushed brother.
Eagerly he seizes that hand, caresses it, kisses it. . . .but over the gulf that separates us.
When I want to draw him gently closer, he backs away,
    for in his other hand he carries his secret,
    too heavy for him to hand to me.
Lord, he hurts me.
I look at him from a distance, and cannot get near him,
He looks at me and cannot come closer.

We both suffer.

He suffers the most, and I can hardly bear it,
   for my love is too limited,
Lord and each time that I try to span his solitude,
   my bridge is too short and does not touch his shore.
And I see him, on the edge of his suffering, hesitating,
   getting set, but drawing back again in desperation,
   for the distance is too great
   and the burden is too heavy.
Yesterday, Lord, he leaned towards me, said a word—
   then took it back: his whole body quivered
   with the weight of the secret
   which approached his lips but rolled back again
   to the depths of his solitude.
He did not cry, but I wiped off big drops of perspiration
   beading his forehead.
I cannot take his burden from him,
He must give it to me.
I see it, and I cannot grasp it.
You do not want me to take it, Lord,
   since he does not want that.

I have no right to violate his suffering.

I am thinking tonight, Lord, of all the isolated ones:
Of all those who are alone, utterly alone,
Because they have never let go
  and been carried by anyone,
Because they have never given themselves to you, Lord;
Those who know something
  that others will never know;
Those who suffer from a sore that no one can ever tend;
Those who bleed from a wound
  that no one will ever heal;
Those who are scarred by a vicious blow
  that no one will ever suspect;
Those who have, locked in the terrifying silence
   of their hearts,
    a harvest of humiliations, despairs, hatreds;
Those who have hidden a mortal sin—cold sepulchres
  behind cheerful fronts.

The solitude of man frightens me, Lord;
Every man is alone, since he is unique;
And that solitude is sacred;

he alone can break through it,
confide and share confidences.
He alone can pass from solitude to communion.
And you want this communion, Lord.
You want us to be united with one another,
In spite of the deep gulf that
   we have dug between us by sin
   you want us to be united
   as your Father and you are united.

Lord, that boy hurts me, as do all isolated ones.
Grant that I may love them enough
   to break through their isolation.
Grant that I may pass through the world
   with all doors open,
My house entirely empty, available, welcoming.

Help me to withdraw so as to embarrass no one,
That others may come in without asking,
That they may deposit their
   burdens without being seen.
And I'll come, silently, to get them by night,
And you Lord, will help me to bear them.

(Abbé Michel Quoist, "Prayers Of Life", Gill & MacMillan, 1954, pp. 44-46)

✠

Reviewing my old essay on the Doctrine of Man, I am almost embarrassed by some of the comments that it contains. We have certainly moved a long way from those days. Of course, I console myself by recalling that I was writing about the understanding of these things from the perspective of some 3,000 years ago and recognize that they were views held by a primitive and struggling nation. It is disturbing how many of those views still hold sway in the minds of some segments of society. It was particularly difficult reading this sentence, "*Man by himself is a complete being and woman adds nothing to his nature. Woman owes her existence to man. The place of woman is in the home—as a helpmate to her husband.*"

In those somewhat primordial days, there simply was no carefully studied and considered belief concerning the complexities of human nature. With respect to the question of procreation it was commonplace at that time to view women as being analogous to an oven or receptacle in which the male seed was incubated to produce new life. Obviously, it would be unfair to judge those views by the standards of modern biology. The ancients certainly realized what needed to take place in order to produce children but had not the benefit of the knowledge that procreation was a joint effort—the uniting of a sperm and an egg when conditions permitted that to happen.

Attempting to produce a meaningful timeline of our understanding of human life would perhaps be a fruitless endeavour. It would be best to touch briefly on a few high points in this attempt to understand who we are and what God expects of us.

In the Middle Ages the Scholastic theologians were quite aware of the importance of understanding human destiny and nature. St. Thomas Aquinas, perhaps the most notable person of the era, was deeply concerned about the nature of being human, especially as creatures of a benevolent God. He had many extremely carefully defined theological opinions about many things including the question of conception—when did a human's life really begin?

This would most certainly not be mentioned by the Roman Catholic Church, in spite of its frequent harking back to Thomistic theology. However, the legacy of Thomas Aquinas's scholarship is undoubtedly what inspires the current level of thought in official Roman Catholic teaching, except that in recent thinking the notion of "life beginning from the moment of conception" has rather abandoned Aquinas, and it seems to be also the view of fundamentalist Christians. This unfortunately leads to extreme exercises in hair splitting as well as proving to be a major assault on the rights and freedoms of women.

At the time of writing we are now approaching the November 2012 election season for the United States. Being so interconnected by our very long and relatively undefended American-Canadian border, and the interchange of television coverage, we cannot really escape being drawn into both the unsavoury aspects of each other's dirty laundry, but also the issues which arise as two parties vie over the affections of the American populous. I will avoid even approaching my thoughts about a two party system, which seems to do nothing more than divide people into two competing mindsets quite apart from the issues that are important for the average citizens who constitute the vast majority of Americans.

One of the colossal issues at this time appears to be one related to our topic—the nature of human kind. It emerges as the problem of abortion that has pushed people of differing opinion into untenable situations on right and left. There are daily newscasts documenting all of this highlighting the completely incongruous views of those who would wantonly do away with the problem people in society to those who maintain that the moment a sperm and an egg come into contact that it is a person with inalienable rights. This leads people, some of whom seem to believe they have some kind of God-endowed, elected responsibility, to make pronouncements about human life with respect to rape, and try to link it to some sort of quasi-religious base.

There has been a very strange change of position during my lifetime with regard to the Catholic faith. To me, the attraction to the catholic faith was to give strong assent to and stress on sacramentalism, spirituality related to the wider church—Our Lady, the Saints, and the Mass. Now it appears that catholic primary issues seem to be fixated on microscopic things and biological notions such as contraception, the rights of the unborn, abortion, and the suppression of women and whoever they might consider to be sexually disordered.

The rights of the unborn is in itself a very legitimate question, however, when it is taken to ridiculous extremes it can verge upon the humorous. I mean defining a fertilized egg as a human being from the very instant that an egg meets up with a lucky sperm is firstly an impossibility to determine and not very helpful, even putting aside the fact that Thomas Aquinas—the great Doctor of the Church—in his *Summa Theologica*, himself gave some wriggle room as to when quickening, or ensoulment, happened. He followed Aristotle with his theory that this took place after a 40-day period from conception for boys and 90 days for girls, which is curious enough in itself. This has all recently exploded as a *personhood* issue—a brand new invention that seems to be appealing to unenlightened Catholics, Republicans and the lunatic fringe of Protestantism.

The gap is narrowing so dramatically that I would not be at all surprised if politicians and theologians did not soon decide that not only is the fertilized egg a sacred entity or person, but that the component parts, the sperm and the egg, were not also endowed with sacredness and mystery in light of their potential. I can picture such people becoming deeply concerned about the millions of parking lots and country drives which are nightly littered with millions of condoms full of these tiny, wriggling would-be humans.

Surely, there must be some kind of intelligent approach to the issues of contraception and abortion that would, on the one hand value and protect human life and yet on the other hand recognize that this is a frightfully complex question which cannot possibly be handled with such a facile and simplistic approach. Fetishism over microscopic life simply does not square with the fact that these same people seem to have no qualms at all in sending off fully developed teenagers and young adults to be slaughtered and maimed in senseless political wars which are often rooted in anxiety about oil or national hubris. If they did take war and its carnage seriously one might be moved to view all the altruistic bluster with considerably more sincerity.

THREE

THE DOCTRINE OF THE CHURCH
Systematics III
February 15, 1968

It is the opinion of numbers of people that the Christian Church has not spent enough time thinking about the doctrine that she holds concerning Herself—the Body of Christ. In an age when we are faced with division and ecumenical encounter we must have some positive idea of just what the Church is and how Christians of varying traditions can come to understand one another.

The concept of the Church goes far back into the history of the Hebrew people and even perhaps further back. They understood themselves to be the "Chosen People" of God—those who had been selected to respond to Yahweh. The Church is prefigured in the Old Testament in many ways, one of which is related to the suffering of Christ. [It will be brought out presently how the Passion, Death and resurrection of Jesus is intimately bound up with the whole concept of the Church.]

The importance of God's intervention into the history of man is seen clearly in the way He delivered the Israelite People from bondage in Egypt and how He continually watched over them and guided them. God's action in history is one of the distinctive features of the Hebrew and Christian religions.

In the Servant Songs of Second Isaiah one can see the most obvious connection between the Passion of Christ and the life of the People of God. The Servant, in this context, is an individual or perhaps the whole nation—it is really a point to be debated—but still this idea of the suffering of one [or of somebody] for the whole, is vividly brought out. It is obedience to God that leads the Servant to his suffering and it is the same thing, which leads Jesus to the Cross. This Servant suffers unspeakable pains of body, and in his innocence, he enables men to be delivered from sin and come into a proper relationship with God. This certainly is the Church's teaching about the work of Jesus.

Jesus fulfilled the scriptures. He went about healing and caring for the outcasts, and finally he was taken and killed.

Jesus' work on the cross completed the prophesies of Isaiah and of the Suffering Servant. He gave Himself a ransom for many. Mankind therefore owes a tremendous debt to Him, and it is in a sense because of this relationship that the Passion of our Lord is inseparable from the concept of His Body—the Church. We find references to the Passion in the Psalms and throughout scripture. Whether or not the particular writers such as Job, Jeremiah, Habakkuk or Isaiah had a clear concept of the suffering of one particular person does not matter. What matters is that through the development of history God acted and gradually things fell into place—and He revealed Himself to men and gave Himself for men.

Fulfilment is recognizable on every hand. Evil was gradually dealt with and eventually Christ won the victory! And through the victory that Jesus effected for mankind, a new Israel was founded—the Church of God—the "Called-Out". God is still active in the world through a People. The Church shares in the Death and Resurrection of Jesus and in a sense the Church has sprung from Jesus' death. In the Sacraments of Baptism and the Eucharist we share again in the Death of Christ and in the Eucharist especially we 'show forth the Lord's death till He come.' By means, then, of Jesus' death, which undoubtedly appeared to be the apex of degradation and failure, we are able to have fellowship with Him and with one another.

In the Marcan account of the Crucifixion, Jesus is completely alone. The Jews misunderstand Him; the Romans thought He was a madman; His disciples cannot understand why He must die; and the thieves crucified along with Him revile Him—yet in His death we glory. It is of course through the victory over sin, which binds and hardens the hearts of men, that we are brought into union with Christ and the Father. Thus we are identified with Jesus' body. The Church, thus, is closely identified with the Death and Resurrection of Jesus.

In New Testament language the People of God are called the εκκλεσια from which is derived the word 'ecclesiastical'. The Church constitutes those who are "called out". It is interesting to see how the continuity with the past was carried over into the Christian Church. The twelve Apostles of our Lord were analogous to the twelve tribes of former years.

In Pauline theology we also see the teaching of the Body of Christ and of the "called out" community. The use of the word σωμα, or body needs perhaps a little explaining. It is used by Paul not in the sense of a group or organization of people, but is used in a much wider sense than that. In his thinking there was not the dichotomy between the 'body' and the 'soul', which seems to have restricted the thinking of some. For Paul they were not opposites. He speaks of bodies of the flesh and spiritual bodies. At any rate, the 'body' of the Church was certainly not simply a group of people or a society. The life of the Christian was intimately bound up with the life of Christ and a participation in His death. Paul wrote to the Corinthian Church, which had apparently experienced various types of problems and admonished them that they must not cause splits in the Body of Christ. Some had apparently followed after Apollos, some after Paul and some after Christ, and Paul implores them, "Were you baptized into the name of Paul? Was Paul Crucified for you?" This sort of thinking would be a breaking of the Body of Christ.

For Paul, the Body of Christ and the Christian life are corporate. The σωμα του Χριστου is physical, glorified, Eucharistic and it is Christ's Church. II Corinthians 5:14 points out that we are convinced that because one died for all, therefore all have died. We all share in the death of Jesus.

In the Eucharist, the sacrament of unity, we see the teaching of the one body and the one blood, and the one loaf and the one cup. There is a common sharing of the Body of Christ. The Body, then, is not some philosophical concept, but it is a visible body of Christian people living in the world.

In the New Testament the structure is present in the apostolic teaching and fellowship and in the breaking of bread and in the prayers of the faithful. Faith and order are really given together in the New Testament and it is not appropriate to try to somehow extract the one from the other.

It is no mere guess that Jesus identified Himself with the Church, His Body. When Paul encountered Jesus on the road to Damascus, Jesus asks, "Why do you persecute me?" We must always remember that in the Bible there are certain ideas that are presupposed and that every detail is not spelled out explicitly. The whole concept of authority is seen in this way. Jesus revealed Himself to His disciples and made it quite clear that He and the Father were one. He also gave them authority to represent Him in the fullest sense. "He who receives you receives me... and "whose so ever sins you remit they are remitted!" These words are certainly a testimony to the complete identification that Jesus made between Himself and His Church. The whole ministry of healing and teaching in the Church was delegated to the apostles and is of course intimately connected with the life and death of Jesus. The Church was thought of as a royal Priesthood and a Holy Nation in much the same way that the Hebrews were specially called and elected. It must always be remembered however that the Church as the Kingdom of God only constitutes the Kingdom of God in a partial way—there is more to the Kingdom than just the visible Church. Christian groups that have overstressed this aspect of the Church's nature have unfortunately gone quite off the orthodox track. The Church is surely composed of ordinary human beings who are sustained by the love of Christ, but who are completely capable of making mistakes and do so all the time. Archbishop Michael Ramsay says that we should look at the Church from the point of view of "not what the Church ought to be but what it is". The importance of being intimately bound up with the Death and Resurrection of Jesus is that the Church is constantly dying to self.

We have seen then that continuity with Christ through the order of the Church is vitally important. But what of groups that have apparently lost visible contact with the Historic Church and still appear to be flourishing? How are we, who put a great deal of importance on such visibility, to regard them? And of course, how does all this fit into the whole question of ecumenism? Something more concrete may come out when we discuss the differences and similarities that exist in connection with the Catholic and the Protestant approaches.

Jesus explained to His disciples that they would not really understand all that He said about His death but that they would have to first share in it—and this is what the Church must present to the world—the scandal, or stumbling block of the Gospel the Death and Resurrection of Christ the Saviour. And the Church will gradually move toward its death and eventually toward its "new life" in Christ, just as Jesus went about ministering to the sick and healing as He moved toward His Death, Exaltation and Resurrection. The important teaching of the Church then, is dying to self. The work of the Christian Church is to point beyond particular theologies and union schemes to the Cross-- and toward the death of the Messiah.

The whole question of Ecumenical relations is associated with the Doctrine of the Church, since the basic foundation of the Church's teaching and administration is tied up in the concepts that people hold regarding the nature of the "Called Out Community". It would be quite wrong to assume that there were simply two basic views, but for the scope of a paper such as this we can only go into a certain amount of detail. Therefore we shall look at the groups of churches that hold a typically 'catholic' point of view and those which follow the Protestant tradition. Perhaps the word 'tradition' here is out of place, since it seems to be such a bone of contention in any discussion of this nature. On the other hand it would probably be good to look at the whole concept of tradition right now since it has presented itself. For quite some time people have intimated that the more 'catholic minded' Christians put their faith in tradition to an unnecessary degree. On the other hand, Protestants have striven to steer away from any mention at all of tradition. In reality, it would probably be more in line with the truth if we recognized that both groups put their faith in tradition, but in two very different traditions.

For the catholic minded Christian, history and God's action within it is a very important concept. God has intervened in history to deliver the Hebrew People from bondage, to make Covenant with His People, to inspire the Prophets, to come to earth in the Incarnation, to heal, teach and to establish the Church. He also continues to make Himself known in the lives of men—even after the close of the New Testament period.

Thus we can see how the institution that Jesus establishes—the Church—is so important to the catholic. Of course this Institution is not merely a structure to further the organizational work of the Church but is a mystical community—the Body of Christ. It is a visible community, which hands on the faith to those who follow in a definite succession. It is this corpus of faith which is handed on which is really tradition. Those who are commissioned by the whole Christian community to continue the work of the Church are certainly ordinary men who are capable of making mistakes. They are fallible. This is something that is often seen in a very different light by people who oppose the catholic point of view. On the other hand there have been periods in history where catholics have presented the faith in such a way that it would appear that the Bishops and Priests (and Popes) are inerrant.

In the same way, any member of the Church is prone to error, but the Church as a whole is beyond reproach in that it is in essence the Body of Christ. In addition, the Sacraments play an essential role in the lives of catholics. By this means God's grace is conveyed to man. The Mass is of course the central offering of the Christian Community. Bishops are the bearers of authority in the catholic structure. The stress in the catholic churches is then on the faith of the Church rather than on the faith of the individual. The community is of prime importance.

The Classical Protestant point of view differed somewhat from this stand. Here we can speak best of the Lutheran and Calvinist groups, as they were the first of the splits with the Catholic Church. They represent the Reformed tradition rather than the marked changes that have been wrought on that tradition since the time of the Reformation. Here again we have used the word 'tradition'. The same ideas that are held to be important regarding tradition in the catholic sense were found in the typically Protestant tradition. They cherished the concept of justification by "faith alone" for instance and the presence of God in the Church aside from what were undoubtedly considered to be mechanical means. This is the Protestant tradition and it is really astonishing that some have attempted to argue that the Protestant Churches do not put any stock in tradition. But, more on this question later!

The Protestant point of view holds that the Church is not above judgement—it can make errors. Neither is the Church self-authenticating, but is rather the servant of the word of God. The Church to these good people is founded on the Word (Christ), which predated the Church and everything else. This is, at any rate, the way the Reformation thinkers saw it. (Perhaps now we find Protestants who have gone quite beyond Reformation thinking and have added tainted layers to their views.) Christ is that Word and the preaching office is the most revered aspect of the Protestant tradition. This is evident even in the architecture of most Protestant Churches. The sacraments are seen in a symbolic rather than a tangible way.

Authority in the Reformed Church comes from below rather than from above in a hierarchical structure. The congregation is the basic unit. Certain Protestant groups see the Church as a community which has fellowship in the Spirit, which is good, but perhaps this idea is pushed beyond its logical necessity. Communion and the other sacramental rites are simply a testifying to the spirit that is already there.

As to the catholic point of view again for a moment, we must mention the teaching of the Church regarding the boundaries of the Church. In the New Testament there is no concept of differing 'Churches'—the word εκκλησια is used to mean the whole church or any part of it, which is really at one with all other parts. There are various points of view on the subject. The Roman Church regards Herself as 'the Church'—meaning, the True Church. Anyone not in communion with that body is outside the Church. At least that is the point of view as we see it in the encyclical Mystici Corporis Christi. More recent literature from the Roman Church seems to regard anyone not in communion with Rome as being deficient, but perhaps in some sense a part of the Church in a much broader concept. Anglicans, although there are certainly groups that are considered somehow deficient and with which there is not intercommunion, do consider other Christians to be part of the Body of Christ. Many of the more traditional Reformed Churches regard all Christians to be part of the Universal Church and do not bother about the problems of intercommunion. On the extreme end of the scale there are radical protestants who, although they probably do not have formal concepts of who is in communion with them and who is not, would regard for instance the Roman Catholics as not being Christian at all. Some of them, in fact, do not even consider Anglicans to be Christian.

POSSIBLE RECONCILIATION BETWEEN CATHOLIC AND PROTESTANT

There are of course certain things that catholics and protestants have in common. Both claim to be followers of Jesus Christ and both value and hold to a spiritual interpretation of the universe— believing God, through Jesus Christ, to be the Creator. Both firmly believe in the process of Redemption through Christ. To a certain degree, both catholics and protestants share in a common experience as to the place of God and the forgiveness of sins. Both have connections with history but, naturally, this is regarded in rather different ways. The Bible is also a close tie. The very scriptures, which protestants hold to be the word of the Lord, form the structure of the catholic liturgy, which is the Truth, and the foundation of catholic life. These are all points where catholics and protestants have a certain measure of agreement and it is on these concepts that they will have to come to a common understanding.

There are, at the same time, as many if not more points of difference between the protestant and catholic views of the Christian Church. One of the main differences between them is one of temperament and a completely different outlook on life. The catholic mystical approach to life is contrasted with the typically protestant ethical approach. The structure of authority within the Church is also crucial, as I have pointed out. Authority from above as opposed to authority from below marks quite a separation. Both catholics and protestants agree basically that God has given some form of ministry—but sorting out that problem is equally quite a chore.

It is interesting that to a large extent, birth has a major role to play in what branch of the Christian Church one belongs to. That two men who hold the particular views that they do because of an accident of birth, and that they should fight tooth and nail because of it, is a truly disturbing proposition.

Because of our basic prejudices and assumptions we often cannot see beyond our particular forms. Both catholics and protestants hold that the Church is not merely an organization run on a series of rules that Jesus set down but that Christianity is the followup of Jesus' having broken into history and reached out toward man. This fact is what we have to keep continually before us when discussing unity. Being able to see truth and value in each other's beliefs and ways is sometimes very difficult but that is what must happen. All have at some time or other emphasized some aspect of the faith out of proportion so that others felt it necessary to seek change; this is why we experienced a Reformation; that is why in the context of the Anglican Communion it was necessary to have a Methodist Movement. The Roman Church had overstressed the Eucharist above other aspects of the faith and this led to difficulties. Archbishop Michael Ramsay says that if episcopacy, the Mass, Baptism or any other of the things that the Church holds important and essential is stressed in isolation, then there is likely to be abuse.

One quite amazing fact that perhaps we should consider is that long before the

Reformation there were men who radically disagreed with one another and yet they remained in communion with one another within the same body. An example of this is the encounter between St. Augustine and Pelagius. Pelagius was of course branded a heretic in the end but for some time they we able to hold quite differing views and remain part of the same body. This issue is very much like the one that still separates Catholics from Protestants. The overstressing on either side of the issue will surely not assist in coercing either God or man to act.

I do not propose to have any idea of how this dilemma can be worked out except to say that it will require much talking and much prayer so that Christians of whatever stripe can come to understand and appreciate the things that their fellow Christians hold dear.

In discussing church structure, for example, Anglicans and Roman Catholics should be able to quickly get to business and identify the points that raise questions, because we have a common vocabulary and similar views. There are still however, points that would appear to be somewhat difficult to resolve. But in Anglican encounters, for example, with bodies such as the Southern Baptist Church there is a vast bridge to close since they do not even think in terms of a wider communion. They are bodies independent of each other with only loose ties, or perhaps, churches rather than a Church.

The most obvious plan of action as far as I see it would be for bodies that have most in common to be the first to seek union and then address the task of dealing with the larger gaps last. Perhaps some gaps will never be closed—at least in this world! This is the principal reason why I feel that talks between the Anglican Church and the Roman Catholic Church should begin long before talks with the United Church of Canada. They in turn would probably be wiser to be deliberating with American Methodists and Presbyterians.

THE PARISH COMMUNITY

On a very practical level, how do we in the Parish situation communicate our ideas and the Church's teaching regarding the Body of Christ?

It seems that this feeling of belonging to the Body of Christ and being in a right relationship with Him is something that cannot be read in a book or communicated by correspondence or even taught. It is a feeling that one gains by experience, as the good Archbishop says by sharing in the Death and Passion of our Blessed Lord. We as future priests will have to be able to communicate the Love of God to people in every way that we can imagine. First, by teaching properly the Church's message through the Word and Sacraments and somehow through personal sincerity and devotion expressing in various ways how we feel about life in the Church.

To those people who see the Church simply a moral policeman we will have to stress the importance of being in communion with a real and concerned God who is our Father, and to those who do not see the purpose of a church that has nice platitudinous teachings, but which does not seem to have anything to say to a torn and unhappy world we must get across the idea that the Church needs to be concerned and do something—perhaps also getting people doing something—more than simply having bake sales and nice committee meetings.

Aside from our relationship with God, our example and our teaching, I cannot imagine any brilliant bookish theories that will help others to catch a glimpse of Christ and fully develop as members of His Body. Perhaps I should have added common sense to the list of things we should strive to do. It goes, of course, hand in hand with the love that we ought to continually demonstrate to all people.

Fr. Donald Andrew Dodman

REFLECTIONS ON THE DOCTRINE OF THE CHURCH
April 2012

To be blunt I found this essay to be somewhat wandering, disjointed and not a little embarrassing. I would probably have given it a 55%, or perhaps a C- or worse had I been the tutor! It certainly reflected my naïveté and nescient ideas about church history and theology and is without a doubt rambling, if not a little pietistic. However, in a vain attempt to give it a tiny bit of credibility, it does provide an entry into the whole miasma of issues that are now throwing the Church into a state of chaos.

In 1965, after a few years of wandering and exploring, I finally made up my mind about what I really wanted to do with my life—and that was definitely to be a priest. After high school there had been a year in which I worked as a teller in a bank to save money to do my first year at university. Then I began a three-year stretch of pre-theology studying general arts and classics at the University of British Columbia. Those were very difficult years for me because I was preoccupied with and even distressed in trying to come to grips with my sexuality. How I envied those who simply accepted who they were and appeared to be quite at peace with themselves.

I had, since my teen years, been involved in the Anglican parish in my neighbourhood, St. Andrew's, Broadview, and at that time the brooding had not yet become much of a distraction. It was during that time also when I discovered St. James, an Anglo-Catholic parish in the skid-road part of Vancouver, which had a marvellous standard of social outreach, liturgy and music. That did uphold me during the darker moments and of course it is the sort of place where there was an accepting and comfortable ambiance. Little did I realize that one day I would serve in that parish myself.

Sometime during my brooding period I toyed with the idea that I might have a career in music. I had played the violin from quite an early age and was truly interested in baroque and classical music. I spent one year with the department of music programme at UBC and it happened that it was the worst year of all for me in terms of my struggle with personal problems. I eventually, with the help of the university medical centre and a very forthright doctor and therapist, came to somehow shake off the doldrums.

At that time I again picked up on my earlier desire to enter seminary, having in a sense, put away the baggage. All that is by way of setting the scene for the events that were to shape my three years of studying theology.

In September of 1965 I entered the Anglican Theological College of British Columbia. I had actually lived at the college, as an arts undergraduate student some years before, so I knew it well and quite loved the life of the college with its round of daily worship, meals and fellowship. The communal living and the ordered life were certainly what I needed and cherished. Since the time I had last lived there, a new residence wing and chapel had been added. It was a pleasant complex and was much in the style of an Oxford college with a quad, dining hall, and common rooms as well as the student rooms. There were other church related theological faculties grouped in that part of the UBC campus and our college had an arrangement with the United Church college whereby we took some Old

Testament and apologetics courses there while their students came to us at ATC for Greek and certain New Testament classes. It was an agreeable situation and Union College was only a stone's throw from ATC.

At some point during that first year, all of a sudden something quite unexpected happened, which for some was thought to be a life-changing crisis, especially those destined for ordination. The Anglican Church of Canada and the United Church issued a discussion document called *The Principles of Union*. I suppose the two churches had been in talks for some time although many of us had not known it. But now, there it was on paper. It caused quite a lot of consternation amongst our students, particularly among those who were of an Anglo-Catholic leaning. I recall with vividness the afternoon that the bombshell hit and all the panicked rhetoric that spread through the college. Before we knew where the discussion was heading or anything about time-frames, some students were threatening to go to Rome or to simply put their plans on hold. There was great scrutiny of this new document and some heated discussions about many of the things it was proposing, particularly regarding questions of authority in the proposed new manifestation of the church.

Personally, I don't particularly recall being in a panic because I felt that these things take much time, debate and negotiation before any life altering decisions are made. Studies continued and I was actually happier than I had been for some years. The work was interesting—fascinating, I might say—and life at the college was certainly what I needed.

We noticed that during the years that followed from time to time there were students from Union College who would come to our Chapel for the daily offices of Morning and Evening Prayer. We knew many of them as we often shared joint classes. In talking with them we were pleasantly surprised that they found the order of Anglican worship helpful. The psalms and biblical readings were set out for the year and the rotation of the church seasons provided a balanced and logical framework for worship which embraced the cycle of the Church's life.

We got over the initial fear that everything we held dear was going to change quickly or worse, be compromised. We were well aware that the United Church of Canada had come about in 1925 with the amalgamation of Methodists, Congregationalists and some Presbyterians.

Consequently, United Church theology and worship tends to be, at least to middle-of-the-road Anglicans and Anglo-Catholics, somewhat thin and even foreign. There were undoubtedly some Anglicans who thought that union with them would be a wonderful thing. However, these things tend to plod on slowly and nothing came of it during the rest of my three years at ATC.

I was made a Deacon in April of 1968 and off I went to work in the world of parish life. For some years wherever I happened to be there were study groups composed of interested people from the local Anglican and United churches meeting together to talk about all manner of church related questions with a view to becoming more aware of each other's traditions. The word *grassroots* seemed always to be a part of the vocabulary of ecumenism. As it happened, the more we talked and got to know one another, the more people were amazed at what each of the churches actually believed and how there seemed to be two completely distinct approaches to the life of the Church.

The one glaring thing that we all noticed was that our structures were entirely different—including how we understood sacraments and especially the theology of holy orders. I had the definite feeling at several points that some of their clergy were rather intrigued with the mystique surrounding bishops, and what's more, that some of them would be rather attracted to that office. In our discussions there were times when that subject would arise and then there would be speculation about how many and which of the United Church clergy would become bishops if the plan succeeded. As I recall, the *Principles of Union* clearly assumed that episcopacy would be a given in the scheme of things. Such conversations also inevitably wandered into the swamps of how we would 'unify' our very different conceptions of ministry. Would we lay hands upon each other and re-ordain each other? Would Anglican bishops have to ordain United Church ministers as presbyters? Talk about apples and oranges! And that was just the beginning of the thorny questions as we stepped into the twilight zone.

How would scripture come into the equation? Anglicans had not really been obsessed with that question—at least it didn't seem so. There were bishops, deacons, and presbyters in scripture, (at least in the Authorized version) and they were all ministers in the general sense, so one of the frequently asked questions was what exactly was a United Church minister? Also, within the framework of the United Church view of theology, a layman could be licensed or given authority to preside at the Lord's Supper. So what did ordination actually mean to them? It appeared to be more focussed on academic credentials. The further we talked the more muddy it all seemed to get.

In 1975 the Anglican House of Bishops rejected the document *Plan of Union, as it had by then been named,* as unacceptable and that was the end of it. They didn't really want to give any concrete reason for this rejection, perhaps so as not to make the situation worse than it had already become. From the rumour mill and unofficial information that I was able to paste together gave the distinct impression that although they had hoped that 'grassroots' discussion would bring people together, it actually seemed to have had the opposite effect and exposed more glaringly how different we were, the result being that we were actually moving farther and farther apart. To me it sounded like it was another of those well-meaning ideas, hatched around boardroom tables in Toronto, which simply went awry. I confess that when it was finally put to rest there was an unambiguous sigh of relief—at least in some quarters. Little did we realize that in thirty or so years the Anglican Church itself would undergo a rather chaotic unravelling.

Somewhere in that framework of time, talks had also begun between the Anglican Communion and Rome with the ARCIC (Anglican—Roman Catholic International Commission) process. They continue to this day although no one expected these talks to achieve anything very swiftly if at all. One of my former bishops used to remark how, with regard to Rome, things frequently take centuries to unfold.

✠

From those observations and impressions of the state of the church in the 1960s and 70s I would like to make a jump ahead a few decades to more recent events. For some curious reason there has been an explosion of opinion and thought in the Anglican Communion during roughly the past ten years. I can't claim to understand why it has happened all of a sudden—perhaps it is simply a quirk and is not confined only to Anglicans. It seems to be erupting in many churches and even in some sectors of secular society. We see this played out nightly on the news channels, especially at this time when elections are dominating news in the U.S. and in Canada, to say nothing of how the recession has affected the entire world. But, curiously, the focus, particularly in North America, is not about economics as much as it is about morality, and more specifically about sexuality. Why are people, mainly heterosexual people, becoming so genitally aware? Perhaps it has to do with the rise of awareness of human rights or the fear that there may even seem to be too many human rights to cope with all at once.

Or is it simply curiosity about what people might get up to in their spare time? Heterosexual people, one would think, might possibly realize that others may be wondering just what variations on a theme they might get up to, aside from simply engaging in uncomplicated sex with the objective of conceiving. That question—conceiving—always seems to lie at the heart of their concern, although perhaps it is because they find a sense of discomfort about things anal. That might in itself be raised as a question for heterosexual people to think about based upon statistics that various studies have revealed. The very percentages involved could make the recreational activities of gay people seem a little insignificant.

The impact of this phenomenon has struck the Christian world a mighty blow, I am afraid. In order to put things into perspective, I am going to try to distil the events that have been happening in the Anglican world during this past decade into a sort of time line. Curiously, almost all of it has happened since my retirement fifteen years ago. I voraciously follow all the news of such things and it will be quite a task to set out what has been going on over those years because almost every day brings yet another twist to an ever writhing controversy. I believe that most of this dispute is rooted in a perverted sense of Puritanism rather than being theological—but then, how ever does one really separate the two.

As I explained in my autobiography, *A Priest's Tale*, I had a strange premonition around 1996-7 that there was going to be some sort of disruption in the church. I thought, in a foggy sort of way, that it was going to be related to the question of authority and the episcopal structure of the Anglican Church. I began to review my finances on a spreadsheet and considered how much I would have to relinquish by taking retirement five years early. Everything seemed to indicate that with my investments and pensions, including what I would forfeit for taking early retirement and giving up my car, I could manage. That began my retirement which has resulted in a number of extremely happy situations including meeting my soul-mate, living in comfort in the city I love, and turning my retirement into a time of writing and simply living life to the full.

With reference to my autobiography, I must make a confession of sorts. Near the end of that book, in its manuscript form, I originally launched out with a laundry list of my pet peeves and expounded on them at some length. As it was rather a different sort of writing from the rest of the book, I titled that last chapter 'Appendix'. I took some heat for that from my partner Devan, who always referred to that part as *The Rant. There were other* people as well who kindly assisted as readers. One of them was our friend James Wright who met me at a local coffee bar to go over the text. He had his copy with him, bristling with yellow, sticky Post-Its and we launched into it. He is an extremely busy man and I was truly grateful for his input. His thoughts and suggestions were indeed significant. I had learned as a parish priest that when you need a volunteer for anything whatever, "always ask the busiest person" and it will be accomplished. When we got through most of the text and reached the 'Appendix', Jim, I sensed, became slightly nervous, as though he thought he might offend me, however he continued......"now this Appendix—don't call it an appendix! no one will read an appendix. It needs to be worked into the body of the text". He was absolutely right—others had articulated the same thing—and eventually I changed it and in the course of doing so I also cut the length of it by about 75%. However, this present volume is, in a sense that same rant, only magnified and detailed many times over. This book could be considered a sequel to *A Priest's Tale even though they are completely independent.*

Now, in order to extract the principal events of the Anglican drama—it will perhaps be best to capsulize because it is simply too complex to try and explore every detail. I think a little preliminary explanation might assist, as there are a number of strands all exploding simultaneously. Some of the events are actually official, but a lot of it is individuals or small groups trying to influence the situation through the internet and blogosphere.

Before launching into specifics, here is a brief description of how the Anglican Church is structured. The first three centuries after 1534 and Henry VIII went along without much need for meetings or conventions. Dioceses were like small, independent fiefdoms working on their own with their Bishop, under the watchful eye of an Archbishop, keeping a hand on the affairs of the church. It consisted primarily of the British Isles and there were two Provinces, Canterbury and York. Along with the Empire, the church spread to other countries where the church sent chaplains to look after those living abroad. The Anglican Church basically became a worldwide entity because of trade and the colonial interests of Britain.

In the 19th century, something happened which made the worldwide church sit up and take notice. A bishop in Africa, John Colenso of the Diocese of Natal, had written or spoken about a pastoral problem that he was encountering, which involved the admission of people to baptism who were in polygamous relationships, which was a very common situation in Africa. He was a man rather advanced for his time who had a wide knowledge of palaeontology and geology and who had questioned the biblical views on the age of the earth and had also become interested and fairly well versed in the relatively new discipline of biblical criticism. But, what caught the eye of several Canadian clerics was Colenso's desire to make an exception for those who had more than one wife and allow them to be baptized without having to jettison all but one wife as had been the policy of the English Church. It was perhaps some time while communications went back and forth between Canada and Canterbury, but eventually the first Lambeth Conference of Anglican Bishops was called for the summer of 1867.

There had apparently been talk in Anglican circles for some time of the need for communication between the various national bodies. The first conference met at Lambeth Palace, the Archbishop of Canterbury's residence in London. The Lambeth Conference meets approximately every ten years in years ending in eight. At that first Conference there were about 140 bishops present and apparently the Colenso issue caused a considerable uproar. Colenso was not present at the meeting, but attempts were made to remove him from his diocese and he was excommunicated. Another bishop was appointed by Canterbury to the See of Natal.

Fairly recently in the scheme of the things we are discussing, in a spurt of activity, Rome has offered *hospitality* to catholic inclined Anglicans with a programme called *Anglicanorum Coetibus* in which Anglicans as groups would be welcomed and brought into full communion with the Roman Catholic Church while retaining certain of their traditions, presumably a very slightly altered Prayer Book liturgy which would have inserted a few words or phrases that would ostensibly make it more acceptable to Rome. It would also allow married Anglican clergy to keep their wives. It must be noted however, that only those clergy being brought aboard in the initial stages would be able to do so with a clear understanding that celibacy would remain as the standard for others in the future. I believe the concordat, which appears to be evolving as they go, also spells out that Roman Catholic priests who had become Anglicans and then married would not be able to participate in this scheme, which does make logical sense. Married bishops joining the Ordinariate would not be able to become bishops of the Roman Church, but would rather be re-ordained as priests.

One of the ironies of this plan, with regard to the continued use of the Book of Common

Prayer, is that for many of the ultra Anglo-Catholic clergy, the missal on their altars has not been the Book of Common Prayer anyway, but rather the Roman Missal and frequently in the Latin Rite.

From the year of my ordination there seems to have been one divisive issue after the other, which have unfortunately ruptured the church and caused untold angst. It began it seems about the time I was ordained with the introduction of various experimental, contemporary liturgies. Some people talked as though there had never been a revision since the 1549 book although there had been several. In Canada there was a revision in 1959, but there was so little variation from the previous book of 1918 that only a handful of people made any issue of it. When I became an Anglican the 1959 Draft Prayer Book was in use at that very time so I had never really used the book that preceded it. I do recall one man who was very upset that in the new Lord's Prayer it said, "Our Father, Who art in Heaven" instead of which art in Heaven. It was rather comical and discomfiting when he would shout out the word WHICH at that point every time we said the prayer. The man was surely in his 50s then and he was frequently an altar server during mid-week Masses, so this slight disruption was rather obvious. At that stage in my development I simply didn't understand the point of it at all. To me it seemed a rather trivial and arcane issue about English grammar. The problem seemed to be really that something had changed slightly, and in any case, I don't really grasp the difference between 'which' and 'that' in many instances, except when it is an interrogative pronoun. It must be lost in the mists of time.

Then came the ordination of women to the priesthood and later on the inevitable followup of the elevation of women priests to the episcopate. When I was nearing the time of my retirement I had the uncanny feeling that there were going to be more problems ahead, which I thought might involve the question of the authority of bishops since order and discipline seemed to be eroding in Anglican circles. I determined that I was financially solvent enough to take early retirement five years before I reached sixty-five even with the forfeiting of the usual annual portion of my pension, so I followed through on that and took retirement in 1997. Fortunately, at the time of my retirement I was working in a large and established Anglo-Catholic parish in Vancouver and all of this agitation and angst had not caught up with our situation there. The ten years I served at St. James' were wonderful, idyllic and busy—a perfect and pleasant way to conclude my working years.

To my astonishment, three or four years after my retirement the gay issue hit the fan. Could it be that this was what my intuition was trying to tell me? Questions about same-sex partnerships and gay bishops seemed to flood to the centre of attention in many parts of the Anglican Church, and it still rages on, every day bringing yet a new twist on the agonizing fragmentation of the Communion.

In the Church of Rome most of the issues I have raised have also occurred on occasion, primarily in the minds of the workaday clergy and people, because the Vatican refuses to acknowledge any such concerns, in fact the church flatly forbids discussion of these questions particularly with regard to issues of sexuality, celibacy, contraception and women's ordination. So far, the Roman Church seems to have been able to make some sort of accommodation for dissident groups so that at least it appears as though they are keeping the lid on things. Special non-geographic ordinariates and societies are often able to give the illusion of unity and keep dissidents in check, but my feeling is that ultimately the pressure will be too much to bear and the dam will break. Cracks in the dam are already beginning to appear.

It is particularly interesting to me that recently the Pope beatified John Henry Cardinal Newman. It is curious that the timing of this coincided with news of the establishment of Anglican Ordinariates whereby disaffected Anglicans could be taken under the wing of Rome. It was surely a blatantly political move. Those Anglicans who are interested in this proposal have been advised that they could retain their wives if married, be re-ordained and also retain certain elements of Anglican Prayer Book worship, with slight nuance changes—which don't seem to have been spelled out quite yet. I cannot help but believe that this is really a little exercise in one-upmanship.

The reason I find this whole procedure a little curious is that Newman was in many ways a progressive thinker, a prolific and articulate writer and often a critic of the Vatican. One of his works was an extensive essay "*On the Development of Christian Doctrine*", which seems to me to be a little inconsistent with the way Rome thinks. During the preparation for this beatification was to be the removal of Newman's remains to a more dignified setting which would ostensibly make his veneration more accessible. It seems fairly obvious that it was also to get him out of the grave of his longtime friend and companion, Father Ambrose St. John, where Newman had specifically requested to be buried. Amusingly, no remains at all were to be found except metal coffin handles as everything, including bones, had completely disintegrated in the English dampness. One writer intimated that Newman had possibly planned the whole thing intentionally to ensure that his remains could not be venerated.

My thoughts about Newman's relationship with Rome is that even though he converted and was eventually made a cardinal, the Vatican never did quite trust him. The lengths to which some people go in order to keep control, order and tidiness in the church have often been extremely painful for those who dare speak their minds. The Newman question has been meticulously set out in a biography by John Cornwell of Jesus College, Cambridge: *"Newman's Unquiet Grave: A Reluctant Saint"*.

Such has been the lot of many talented and distinguished people including Galileo, Hans Küng,

Pierre Teilhard de Chardin and a French bishop, Monseigneur Jacques Gaillot, who, following his conscience, was treated in a most shoddy and uncivil way. Although remaining obedient to Rome, he has been able to turn his misfortune into something creatively novel.

Jacques Gaillot was appointed to the see of Évreux in Normandy, a little west of Paris, in 1982. He is a visionary man who took seriously the mandate to care for the sick, the poor and the disadvantaged. He was known to be a social activist and began to be involved in situations that eventually led to his removal. During his first Easter message in Évreux Cathedral he said: *"Christ died outside the walls as he was born outside the walls. If we are to see the light, the sun, of Easter, we ourselves must go outside the walls."* After this beginning he added words that indicated that he was convinced he was there to support the ill and serve the lost. He said, "Does a bishop remain in his cathedral or does he go into the street? I have made my choice." Within a few months he began to act on his word.

During his thirteen years as Bishop of Évreux, Monseigneur Gaillot became involved in many causes where human rights were being violated including supporting a conscientious objector who appeared before a court in Évreux to backing the First Intifada in the West Bank and Gaza Strip. He even met with Yasser Arafat in a private audience. In 1987 he attended by invitation a special assembly of the United Nations to speak on the subject of disarmament. On many occasions he angered Catholic authorities by refusing to support the movement in defence of French parochial schools.

Notable attention was paid to the Bishop in 1985 when he signed an appeal on behalf of underpaid Catholic teachers along with Georges Marchais who was head of the French Communist Party. Soon there was a rightwing campaign against the Bishop for being a "tool of the church's worst enemies" as some termed it.

At one point he expressed his views before a Catholic assembly in Lourdes where he advocated the ordination of married men to the priesthood. His openness to the press was also a thorn in the side of the Catholic hierarchy. To do this was to violate conventions, which the Vatican holds to vigourously. Eventually the time came when he openly promoted an evaluation of clerical celibacy and the use of condoms. This caused an uproar within the French bishops' conference, and his response apparently was, "I never broke my vow of celibacy, I only questioned it."

A string of events followed, including his blessing of a same-sex couple who were both in immanent danger of death by AIDS, and a visit to Polynesia organized by a peace movement asking for the termination of French nuclear testing. He had earned an impressive reputation, both positive and negative. One French journalist, Henri Tincq wrote in Le Monde, "Bishop Gaillot has the merit of saying out loud what many people in authority in the church think down deep."

The list of offences charged against Bishop Gaillot grew longer and longer. It is somewhat astounding how he persisted in his quest before finally being disciplined. Eventually, as is so often the case, he began to be attacked personally. He was accused of all the usual things; of being racist, antisemitic, a homosexual and for suffering from psychosis and neurosis, and these emanating from some most influential amongst the French clergy.

In January of 1995, Jacques Gaillot was summoned to a meeting with Cardinal Gantin, prefect of the Congregation for Bishops at the Vatican. He was offered a choice. He could resign his bishopric and become bishop emeritus of Évreux, or be removed from the see. If he chose the latter, he would be assigned to the titular see of Partenia. He chose not to resign. He returned to France and gave a press conference.

Bishop Gaillot was then demoted. He accepted the ultimatum and became the Titular Bishop of Partenia. This is where the story becomes rather amusing and also the point at which the Vatican probably regretted the implementation of that sort of treatment.

The Diocese of Partenia is actually defunct —since the fifth century—and is in the Sahara Desert in Algeria. It was once a large city but is now a tiny wind swept village. Bishop Gaillot took on that responsibility, but with a twist. Since there are almost no people there to deal with (except, possibly a few), the Bishop has taken to dealing with his new diocese as a virtual, internet entity. His outreach has become enormously popular and perhaps has actually been enhanced by the internet component. The aspect of this story, which arrests my attention so deeply, is that there are people who are willing and determined to stand for truth no matter the personal cost. Bishop Gaillot speaks frequently to groups, writes, publishes and continues to be involved with those who dwell on the fringes of society. Many of his fellow French bishops remain in contact with him and have assured him of their support and prayers.

I chose to use the example of Monseigneur Jacques Gaillot to illuminate just what the Doctrine of Man is really about. Throughout the scriptures and the life of the Church there is seen a gradual refining and developing of the place we allot to other human beings. It is seen most fully in the life and words of Jesus the Christ and in the lives of many who follow Him.

I know from personal contacts that many of those who initially found this programme appealing are having second thoughts and I would not be the least bit surprised if the plan was found to evoke scant interest. Rome should surely be aware that most of those attracted to this idea had already departed from the Anglican Church, often decades ago and would be bringing with them plenty of baggage.

Heaven only knows that Rome already has enough of its own dissenters and many of them are just hanging on by a thread. Rome has been rather clever in keeping such groups under the umbrella in the guise of Uniat dioceses or Personal

Prelatures such as Opus Dei, the Society of St. Pius X and the Legion of Christ. The anguish that such groups have brought is public knowledge.

One local community which separated from the Anglican Church of Canada decades ago in British Columbia began to fragment even before any official arrangements had begun with respect to an Anglican Ordinariate. That, I believe, for some was because of the *re-ordination* factor which obviously implies that one's Priestly orders are not considered to be valid, which is of course, Rome's official position.

Anglicanorum Coetibus—the Vatican's name for this process—means something like "Gatherings of Anglicans" but the word coetibus has many implications like "fellowship, association, encounter, gang, band, or social intercourse". There appears to be a close linguistic relationship between the Latin words *coetus* and *coitus*. One of my clerical friends has an amusing translation of what the phrase Anglicanorum Coetibus means in straightforward and earthy English, but I will leave that to your imagination!

As much as Christians talk about the need for unity and solidarity, and as much as we sincerely believe that we should all be one, even as

Jesus and the Father are one, it seems that it is not all that simple. In recent years, just within the Anglican world, there have been literally hundreds of breaks and divisions. Since yesterday, when I mentioned the Roman Catholic move to welcome Anglicans 'back home', I learned yet more about the dynamics of that situation. Although *Anglicanorum Coetibus* might look as though it is healing divisions and bringing unity, it is actually helping to create even more splits. Some in the British Columbia group who were not eager to follow on to Rome set up yet another Anglican jurisdiction attached to a dissident American bishop. That was for some of them the second or perhaps even the third time they had separated from a parent body.

In terms of unity in the church, while there was a small number who were absorbed by Rome, there is still a portion who chose not to go, plus the ones who had already removed themselves. Instead of unity then, where theoretically two groups would become one, there are now three groups instead of two. Naturally, for tiny, struggling churches the numbers game comes into play, but that is hardly a concern for Rome where numbers are claimed to be astronomical. This process is actually now in its initial phase but time will undoubtedly reveal that there are more problems to emerge. From other people's past experience and not a little of my own, Rome will eventually realize that these new acquisitions will have brought all their angst and dissatisfaction along with them.

✠

The nature of the Church is essentially one of unity, 'that they all might be one', allowing that there needs to be room for a certain amount of local expression, liturgically, socially and linguistically. It would perhaps be true to say that there never has been total unity given those restrictions. Even the church Fathers of the first four or five centuries had their disagreements and preferences. However, at this time at the beginning of the twenty-first Century we see Christendom as an extremely wide palette—so wide, in fact, that many would place some of its manifestations quite outside the pale.

Recently, at the time of Pope Shenouda III's death, I saw television coverage of parts of his Coptic funeral mass. In reality that sort of liturgy is probably quite close to the norm for Christian worship in the earliest centuries. Many of the world's Christians would scarcely recognize it as even being Christian, but might perhaps think it to be Muslim or some strange cultic worship. There might be a similar reaction to what I experience when witnessing some of the fundamentalist shenanigans that pass as Christian worship and wonder how far from the basic principles of faith and order some people have moved. I hate to use this cliché but I wonder what Jesus might think about it? It would be most interesting to know, and when I get to heaven (if, indeed, that is where I end up) I will ask about it!

Christianity has obviously changed over the centuries with the various movements and theological positions such as happened at the time of the Reformation, to say nothing of the Anglican break with Rome under Henry VIII.

✠

Four

THE NATURE OF THE EUCHARIST
Systematic Theology III
March 14, 1968

The Holy Eucharist has always been the central act of worship in the Christian Church—at least it should be regarded as such. In an age when Christians are thinking very seriously about unity the eucharist must of necessity occupy much of the time and effort spent by ecumenists since our unity is summed up in this great sacrament which binds the church together and which allows it to have a life in Christ. Communions that have been separated for centuries over issues such as those regarding the nature of the Lord's Supper are finding that with fresh approaches and with real concern they are realizing that the gaps are really not as marked as was once thought.

NATURE OF THE EUCHARIST

Traditionally in the Church the eucharist has been regarded as the sign of and cause of unity within it. The community of Christian people gathered together with the Bishop, the successor to the Apostles, are nourished by the saving Body and Blood of Christ. Various problems arise in any discussion of the eucharist and needless to say one of these is the question of the 'real presence'. Cyril of Jerusalem explains to the neophytes that the bread and wine are definitely associated with the body and blood of Christ. Jesus words "this is my body" are taken seriously and by partaking of His body and blood the Christian becomes a bearer of Christ. The Community is nourished by the body of Christ and it is bound to Christ in this sacrament. Augustine says that in the eucharist one thing is seen but another understood. The eucharist is the sacramental commemoration of the Passion of Christ. In the early Fathers we do not find any formal treatment of this subject other than the fact that they regard Jesus to be really present in the eucharist.

THE PEOPLE OF GOD

In order to fully treat the subject of the eucharist we must first examine for a few moments the concept of the People of God. The eucharist binds and unites the community of the faithful. Back in the early Jewish ethos we encounter the concept of community, the Qahal, as the Chosen People of Yahweh. The forerunner of the Christian eucharist can be seen here. The Qahal was an assembly duly summoned and called together. The head of the community would preside and invoke a blessing over the cup. This thanksgiving is the ευχαριστεω. It is the κηρυγμα or the proclamation of the Word of God, which ultimately calls the community together, and it is communion with God that is the object of the gathering.

There has of course been endless debate as to just which meal (the 'chaburah' or the 'kiddush') the Christian eucharist was patterned after. However, the important thing is that the eucharist is the gathering of the community in communion with God through Christ. In the Christian liturgy we find both speaking and doing—a holy action. The liturgy of the Word is God's

Word coming down to us. The liturgy is the hearing of God's word. Even in the second part of the liturgy--the Thanksgiving proper—we are participating in God's Word. Men are placed, through the Word of God, into a proper perspective in relationship with the New Creation. Here in the eucharist the Word is made visible. The celebration of the eucharist is not simply the hearing of God's word in the broader sense but it is the situation 'par excellence' in the life of the Christian Church. Here the Bible and tradition are intimately joined together. Eucharist is the final stage of the process of initiation into the Body of Christ, and here the Christian finds constant strength for the battle that lies ahead. It is not simply a set of religious propositions into which we are initiated but rather to a life of prayer and action into which we are called.

THE LITURGY

The word 'liturgy' [λειτουργεια] comes from ancient Greek times and meant public service to one's city. From the time of the Apostles it took on the connotation of taking part in the solemn, corporate worship of God by the priestly society of

Christians. Officially liturgy is all of the organized worship of the Christian Community although it has come to be associated mainly with the eucharist. This corporate action in the eucharist has the seal of Jesus Himself upon it by virtue of His command "Do this in remembrance of Me". In the Sacrament of the Altar Christians are united to the life, work and purpose of Jesus Christ. As early as 96 AD, Clement speaks of the bishops, priests and deacons along with the laity all in their various orders taking part in the liturgy. He makes reference to 'appointed rules" and to 'liturgies' as being Divinely appointed rites.

The eucharist is really an expression "toward God of what the Church really is" (Dom Gregory Dix, The Shape of the Liturgy). The Church is therefore a holy priesthood corporately offering up spiritual sacrifices, which are acceptable to God through Jesus Christ.

Father Eric Mascall says that the eucharist and the catholic Church are inseparably joined. The theological development of the eucharist seems to have gone straight through the Reformation period without really touching the theology of the Church and thus we see it developing as a sort of individual relationship of the believer with God. It is therefore of the greatest importance that we now examine the pre-Medieval doctrine of the Church in order to put things in their correct perspective. The Church is the Mystical Body of Christ and the eucharist is an act of Christ within this Body. This allows a fuller incorporation of His members into Christ; thereby Christ is drawing men to Himself.

In the First Epistle of Peter we see how the Church should be regarded—as "living stones' building up the visible Church. We, as the Church, are to live as a Holy Society—a supernatural and sacramental society—acting and living as a community before we attempt to begin teaching. Thus it is primarily action that we are called to, and other functions follow from this.

In the eucharist all of our sins, failures, misery as well as our love for one another and for God are brought before God and we are brought into a close relationship with Him. All Creation is God's and in the eucharist all of God's possessions are brought before Him in offering. Christ died for all men—and for the whole world—as well as for believers in His son, and thus all things and all people are summed up before

God in the Eucharistic Sacrifice. The Church is the recreated human race—the Holy People of God. Though the Church may be black with the sins of its members, yet it is comely with the beauty of its Head and the sacraments are its very life. In the eucharist we see summed up the oneness of the Church.

SYNAXIS AND ANAPHORA

The very basic core of the Eucharistic service falls into two main parts—synaxis and eucharist. The synaxis is a continuation of the Jewish synagogue service. Early Christians did not cease to worship in the synagogue after they had come to believe in Christ. As Paul and many others continued to attend the synagogue, so the Church saw the value of this worship and made good use of it. One probably should not put it in that way—it sounds like the Church consciously worked things out in this way. It would be more correct to say that the services of the synagogue simply continued naturally into the Christian Church.

The eucharist, and especially the liturgy of the Gifts, was certainly something new. This is not to say that it had never been heard of before because we know that in a sense it evolved from the chaburah meal or perhaps the Kiddush (this is a matter of considerable debate) but Christ placed upon the eucharist a very new meaning.

In early times the synaxis and the eucharist could be, and were most likely often, separated by time and used quite independently. For example in the writing of Hippolytus we see the consecration of a Bishop preceding the breaking of bread or in another place a baptism preceding the eucharist. From about the fourth century we see a fusion of the synaxis and the eucharist and eventually they were always used together as we have today—one unified rite. However, the first part of the Mass still revolves around the book of the Scriptures and not around the altar and the sacred vessels.

The synaxis consisted of scripture, psalms, a sermon or homily, and certain prayers just as the synagogue service did. It seems that at one time the prayers were in a different place (before the sermon) but they were later placed after the sermon and that is where we find them to this day. In the early Church all people were invited to the synaxis or what is sometimes called the Mass of the Catechumens but after the

Eucharist itself began the un-baptized were taken out and only the faithful remained. The catechumens would often receive a blessing from the Bishop before leaving.

The prayers were an integral part of the Mass and the bishops, priests, deacons and laity all took part in them. There would be petitions gathered from the congregation and at the end the celebrant (the Bishop) would weave all of these petitions into a long prayer of intercession. It would be something like our Prayer for the Church. The liturgical movement has tried to revive the idea of collecting petitions from the congregation so that the Mass is an action of the whole people of God and not just something done for the congregation by the priest. The prayer is then an action of the whole community.

THE FOURFOLD ACTION

In the New Testament it appears that at the Institution of the Eucharist there was a sevenfold action. It soon became a fourfold action of, i) offertory, ii) prayer and thanksgiving, iii) fraction and iv) communion. This sequence is actually an invariable nucleus. All of the subsequent eucharistic rites have followed this form; of course, these four things are what Jesus did at the Last Supper. "He took, gave thanks, broke and gave". There were occasional incidents where certain heretics took exception to the use of wine but they still adhered to the fourfold action. (In some cases water would be substituted for wine.)

Dom Gregory Dix feels that the meal being observed at the Last Supper was not the Passover but the meal of the evening before--the chaburah meal. At any rate it was a common meal, which had probably social, and business overtones. By 'business' we mean the business of the particular society—things concerning all present.

The Offertory of the Mass is the offering of our substance to God. As Jesus took bread and wine so we take the fruits of creation and offer them to the Father. This part of the Mass is sometimes called, in technical language, the anaphora, which means "to present or bring up". Again, in the liturgical Movement we see this emphasized and restored in the action of the people bringing the elements up from the congregation to the celebrant. Here we set aside our possessions for God's use. This is an expression of the common priesthood of the laity.

THE EUCHARISTIC PRAYER

The eucharistic prayer has many things in common with the benediction prayer of the Jews. During this prayer the celebrant places his hands upon the oblations and gives thanks to God. Here also we pray for remembrance. Unfortunately the English language gives the impression that we are remembering something that is not present. This part of the Mass is called the "anamnesis". The more accurate sense of the word anamnesis or 'recalling' would be "to make a past event a present reality". In the Mass we have the effectual offering by the Church of the sacrifice of Calvary. Also in the prayer we have the 'epiclesis' or the petition for the descent of the Holy Spirit "that they all may be made one" with one another.

FRACTION

The fraction in the middle ages was seen as a particularly sacerdotal act—the priestly mactation (slaughter for sacrifice) of the victim. This was shared by the presbyters and the deacons. This part of the Mass is of course the same as our Lord's breaking of the bread at the last

Supper. The communion, or the giving of the body and blood, is the administration to the faithful—completing what Jesus did.

The Christian Church is the New Israel and it is indissolubly connected with Jesus—the Church is His Body. This is why in the eucharist the Church is both priest and victim offering herself to God for a savour of sweetness.

Yngve Brilioth, a Finnish bishop and scholar, contends that the eucharist can be divided into four elements. They are: Communion, Sacrifice, Eucharist (thanksgiving), and Memorial.

Communion in his list is not the administration of the sacrament, but rather koinonia, [κοινωνια], a common partaking or a sharing in common goods. Sacrifice is what the Church does when she meets for the celebration of the eucharist. In the Epistle to the Hebrews we see a sacrificial explanation of the Cross. There is a definite connection here with the Old Covenant. But there is another view of sacrifice, which is also present in this context. That is the personal sacrifice of which Paul speaks. For example the Corinthians sacrificed when they sent aid to the Christians at Jerusalem. Paul also speaks of the sacrifices, which he himself has made for the Church.

Thanksgiving during the synaxis is said by the President of the Eucharist and in it he sums up the relationship that exists between the congregation and God—the relationship between themselves, Creation and Redemption. Here the wine and the bread are typical of all Created things. Brilioth speaks of memorial as the memory of the Cross and the Great Saving acts of Christ through which the Divine Agape flowed into the world. It is a memorial of everything, which led to the cross, and this includes not only the words of Jesus but also the sacrifice of Abraham-- the intended sacrifice of Isaac--and the sacrifice of Abel. God's entrance into human history in other words is brought into remembrance. Brilioth also holds that there is a fifth element in the eucharist and that is 'mystery'. This element covers and pervades each of the other four elements.

MAN AND SACRIFICE

There seems to be a very natural tendency for man to desire to sacrifice. Men seem to automatically do this before they even think what they are doing. In the

Bible sacrifice is a normal concept—for modern man the notion is foreign. The word 'sacrifice' is still with us but the real meaning seems to have disappeared. It has been thought of simply as the destruction of a living being but more and more we are coming to understand that it has a far more comprehensive and richer meaning—a more positive meaning.

We often think of sacrifice as a bloody, gory affair accompanied by squeals of torment. Actually the emphasis in sacrifice is not on the death of the victim at all. Fr. Mascall uses the analogy of the Christmas dinner. We all sit around the festive table and in the middle is a carcass. But we are not dwelling on the idea that here is a creature dead—one that has been tormented. We are there to enjoy a meal and fellowship. It is a happy occasion.

In the sacrifices of the Jews the animals were used in the service of God. He is their cause and their final end. God takes sacrifice and transforms it. Man has been created by God and he is to take his life and sacrifice it in filial obedience to the Father. As Fr. Mascall says, sacrifice "is a ritual expression of (one's) ontological status". Rather than offering himself to God in sacrificial death, men began to offer other beings. God does not glory in the destruction, but rather he takes it and transforms it. The sacrifices of bulls and heifers did not remove sins they merely kept alive the fact that there was something else needed to accomplish this end.

As already stated, this idea of slaying has unfortunately harmed the whole idea of sacrifice, especially in connection with the Redemptive work of Christ. Jesus' whole life was a sacrifice and an offering to the Father. His Baptism, Transfiguration, Passion and Resurrection are all part of His saving work. It could be said that Jesus' whole life on earth was a solemn Mass—He being the Priest, Victim, Altar and Temple. In the eucharist the Church is made what she is and Christians are made what they really are.

SACRIFICE IN THE EUCHARIST

The complaint that the Reformation thinkers levelled at the existing doctrine of the sacrifice of the Mass was certainly not without provocation. The Medieval theologians seem to have lost touch with the Jewish and early Christian views of sacrifice. They concentrated only on the aspect of sacrifice, which dealt with the death of the victim. Thus the sacrifice of the Mass became simply a repetition of the death on Calvary. Swinging the other way, the Reformers stressed the "once-for-all" aspect of Jesus' sacrifice. Along with this they almost totally dropped the idea of sacrifice. Because of this trend in thought we are compelled to reexamine the Jewish and early Christian teachings of sacrifice.

For the Old Testament, the death of the victim was merely the first step in a sacrifice with a much wider scope. The sacrificial act enables the sacrificer to enjoy communion with the Father. As has been stated already, in the Epistle to the Hebrews we see Christ as the High Priest, through whom sacrifice is made. He is also the victim. His sacrifice must not be thought of as taking place at a point in time —but rather as something that takes place in eternity. Jesus is still obedient to the Father as He sits at His right hand. The manhood of Jesus is offered for us.

In the New Testament we find that the Messiah is one with his people and through his death there is expiation—guilt is wiped out. In the Gospel of John, Jesus is regarded as the Lamb of God and along with this title goes the whole concept of sacrificial worship. Paul seems to focus on the concept of substitutional atonement. In II Corinthians 5:14 Paul says, "One has died for all; therefore all have died". In the Epistle to the Hebrews sacrifice has taken place once-for-all but its work is valid for all time. Through Jesus' sacrifice a New Covenant is established although the redemptive work of Christ is not finished.

Sacrificial language is also used in other places in the New Testament. Jesus is said to be "given for you" and His blood is said to be "shed for you". This sort of language is used not only in connection with the words of institution at the Last Supper, but in other contexts. In Mark 10:45 we read that He "gave His life a ransom for many". In I Peter 1:18 He is "ransomed with the precious blood of Christ like that of a Lamb without spot." Christ bears our burden in order to establish the New Israel. In order to be able to make this sacrifice for us, Jesus takes upon himself our nature—-He assumes the conditions of sin and death so that he can make atonement for us.

It must be noted that here we do not have a sort of triangle arrangement between God, Jesus and humanity. God does not simply stand idly by while all of this sacrificing is going on. He is actively involved. It was He who sent His Son into the world to do this atoning work.

It is really God's own sacrifice. "God so loved the world....". And God did not simply initially send His son and then let things carry on however they might go. He sent His Son to die and make atonement for our sins. The Death of Jesus was in other words a Divine Necessity. God gave Him as a sacrifice—He did not simply "permit" Jesus to die. God was in Christ reconciling the world unto Himself; he was not simply a spectator.

REAL PRESENCE

Any discussion of the subject of sacrifice must touch somewhere on the topic of the real presence. Tied up in this is the relationship between the sacrifice on Calvary and the Lord's Supper. In the New Testament teaching we see a sort of expectant eschatology. We celebrate the Lord's death till He comes. This sort of language points toward the great supper in Heaven—a rather unfortunate phrase. But we also have a belief in a 'realized eschatology'. Fellowship with Christ is renewed in the eucharist because of the Resurrection and Exaltation. Paul in I

Corinthians 10:14 speaks about participation in the Body and Blood of Christ thus, our taking part in the saving work of the Risen Christ. In the Gospel of St. John (chapter 6) we see the presence of Christ being maintained just as really as if He were in the days of His flesh. St. John uses two words, which certainly seem to indicate that Jesus is really present with reference to the eating of Christ's Body in the eucharist. He uses the word 'trogein' [τρωγειν], which means to chew or masticate. And again when speaking of Christ's Body itself he uses the word 'sarx', [σαρξ], which would indicate a more fleshly presence than if he had used the word σομα, [body].

As already noted, the Reformers seem to have overstated their position on the side of the absence of sacrifice in the eucharist but not without provocation. One writer remarks that they even became negatively dependent on the very theory they rejected. (C.F. Moule). A proper view of sacrifice must then go beyond the scope of the limited view that was popular in the Middle Ages—which is that the sum total of Christ's sacrificial death was the actual death. It must encompass the whole of the life and death of Jesus as well as the whole of the activity of God in history. Sacrifice is not something that is finished—the Word (Λογος) became flesh and remains so—He continues in His heavenly existence.

    Because of the unity between Christ and His Church, the eucharist can be spoken of as the offering of Christ. The act of the Church is Christ's own act and the Church's offering is Christ's offering. The notions of death and sacrifice cannot be separated—a strong emphasis on the one means a strong emphasis on the other. Martin Luther by his views on the real presence emphasized the concept of sacrifice although he did not say so in any explicit way. Christ's sacrifice cannot be thought of as being in a point of time any more than His love for us can be restricted to a point of time—it must be regarded in a much wider sense. The Incarnation could be said to be the starting point of Christ's sacrificial act. It is true that in the New Testament there is an emphasis on the death on the Cross, but this certainly does not minimize the other aspects of Christ's life and His redemptive work. Because Christ is not limited by time and space, sacrifice is effectively present in the Lord's Supper.

In the bread and wine we find the meeting place between the Risen Lord and the People of the New Covenant—the Church. The past becomes then the present, and Christ's death is much more than something that happened around 2000 years ago. Thus it makes sense that we can say that "Christ is offered" or that we "offer His sacrifice". These phrases have caused a considerable amount of anguish in the past. The idea of offering Christ as a meritorious act soon becomes attached to this teaching if we are not careful. His one sacrifice does not need to be complemented by continuous sacrifices.

It is somewhat difficult to give a simple answer to the question "Why do we offer Christ in the Eucharist?" It has been said that through the sacrifice our adoration becomes perfect and we receive a sure proof of the sufficiency of divine redemption. In the sacrifice we see the 'love' of God, not a God who demands to be appeased.

The Eucharist is celebrated at the command of God: "Do this in remembrance of me." Jesus actualizes the sacrifice anew in the eucharist. This sacrifice is a victory and Christ is the Heavenly Victor.

Fr. Donald Andrew Dodman

REFLECTIONS ON THE EUCHARIST
May 2012

During my teen years I became involved in the Anglican parish in my neighbourhood. I had made visits to various other churches within walking distance—United, Pentecostal, Baptist and Congregational. There was no nearby Roman Catholic Church but for some reason I did not then consider that to be within the range of my inquisitiveness. Perhaps it was partly because of my upbringing, even though there was nothing overtly religious or non-religious about that for my family. There were some distant second cousins who were Pentecostal, who to my way of thinking behaved in a peculiar way about almost everything. The mother of that family, Auntie Ethel, who was my grandmother's sister, had been converted at a huge rally that took place at the Pantages Vaudeville Theatre in Vancouver in the 1920s.

It happened during a visit of Aimee Semple McPherson, and when the altar call, or whatever that element of the worship was called, Auntie Ethel, who was sitting in one of the balconies, walked down to Miss McPherson on the stage through the air without benefit of stairs she claimed. We actually had very little contact with that branch of the family except perhaps at Christmastime when there would be a gala dinner at my grandparents' home. I didn't really appreciate all the dynamics of it as I was just a little boy, but I was certainly aware that they were, what shall I say, *different*. My part of the family was really quite secular although my grandparents had been involved in the Anglican Church in New Westminster when they emigrated to Canada in 1910, my grandfather even becoming organist at St. Mary's, Sapperton.

After visiting churches in the neighbourhood I finally felt very much at home and comfortable in the little Anglican church of St. Andrew. The Rector was very natural, friendly and unimposing. The worship was ordered and dignified which appealed to me greatly. It was very much the middle-of-the-road Anglican sort of thing. Of course, at that time I had no real conception of the breadth that existed in Anglican circles.

Confirmation classes with four or five other adults I found to be interesting and informative. I became involved in that parish in so many different capacities—Sunday School teaching, volunteer janitor, altar server, choir member and eventually theological student.

As the confirmation day approached I was curious about receiving communion and about how it might feel. In a sense, I thought that it might be a sort of religious experience. It was truly memorable and meaningful to me, but nothing extraordinary was felt which is completely in keeping with my psyche. I was uplifted in a deeply spiritual way and that connection has remained throughout my life.

Before very long another life-altering event happened to me. A high school friend knew that I had been confirmed in the Anglican Church and he too was being prepared for confirmation. He asked if I might come to the service. He explained that it would be at St. James' Church downtown, but that if I needed a lift his parents would give me a ride as I lived on the route from their home to the church. I had known the family for some years through music and I was happy for the ride as the church was in the depressed area of Vancouver's skid-road where I had never really explored. They picked me up on their way and it proved to be one of the most interesting turn of events in my life.

We entered the imposing concrete, ivy covered church and found a pew. The organ played quiet and devotional music and the smells were tantalizing—beeswax from the candles and the faint smell of incense. The Bishop was escorted in with incense and lights as the service began. He was dressed a little differently than he had been at St. Andrew's—instead of a rochet and chimere (choir dress), an ornate cope and mitre. It was rather glorious. The organ thundered as he was led into the sanctuary. Little did I know that I would someday be on staff in this wonderful place.

At this time in the 1950s, most Anglican Churches in the Diocese of New Westminster offered the celebration of the Eucharist about once a month at the main service. There would often be weekly celebrations early on Sunday mornings, but Matins or *Morning Prayer* was frequently the usual fare at the main Sunday service. At that time there were about four parishes, which employed more catholic practices such as eucharistic vestments and more frequent celebrations of the Eucharist.

It was not long before I was entertaining ideas of the priesthood and I began the process of considering university and life at the Anglican Theological College of British Columbia. To make a long story shorter, seven years later I completed my theological studies and was ready for ordination. (A longer version of that period is detailed in my autobiography).

The Pentecostal part of the family caught wind of this even though we rarely had any social contact, they apparently came to visit my parents to warn them that I was destined for Hell and such dire things. To their credit, my mother and father who were really not all that enthused about my career choice themselves in the beginning, apparently told them to go off and mind their own business.

I was made a deacon in my home parish of St. Andrew and was soon sent off to Northern British Columbia to join a mission team, which served a dozen or so small churches in the Bulkley Valley. Normally at that time one usually remained in deacon's orders for about a year and was then ordained to the Priesthood, but unfortunately Bishop Munn died and there was a delay so that a synod could be called and an election held. Then after that had been decided it took many months before the new bishop was consecrated and for things to settle down. I remained a deacon for something like two and a half years. Finally, when the new bishop came to our mission for confirmations the Priest in Charge and I had a chance to sit down with him to attend to a number of things, one of them being when I might be ordained to the Priesthood.

When asked that question, the bishop responded that perhaps I had a vocation to remain in deacon's orders permanently. He offered nothing more and the discussion simply ended. I should note that at about that time in history a permanent diaconate was thought to be a chic idea. People were trying to justify even having deacons because the order had simply developed into a kind of internship before Priestly ordination. No one quite knew what to do with deacons because in Anglican practice at that time any lay person could do all of the things that deacons did.

But, to return to how all of this relates to the subject of this essay I should explain that my long and frustrating diaconate meant a lot of driving long distances between tiny gatherings of Anglicans taking the pre-consecrated bread and wine in a little wooden box and offering what we used to call "dry masses". I was doing everything a priest would be doing except for consecrating the elements and pronouncing the normal absolution after the General Confession. There was never in my experience an occasion when anyone wanted to make a private confession which I could not have done in any case. I felt quite strongly that this was hardly the ministry for which I had been trained. I eventually obtained a position in another diocese where I was almost immediately ordained to the Priesthood and began to function.

One of the sections in my college essay on the Eucharist dealt with the question of the *real presence—the belief that Christ is truly present in the Blessed Sacrament.* This belief has always been a part of Anglican and catholic theology concerning the elements of the consecrated bread and wine to some degree or other. I recently looked at my copy of the First and Second Prayer Books of Edward VI, 1549 and 1552. These two Prayer Books reflect the reformed ideas of the writers and there seems to be some trouble taken to avoid idolatry on the one hand and yet to respect the depth of the teaching about the Eucharist on the other. There is talk of taking great care that the sacrament is not abused, although I did find one reference that perplexed me a little in the 1552 book. It seems that there was more of a protestant emphasis in this version than in the former.

This rubric from the 1552 Prayer Book, I found to be a little troubling:

"And to take away the supersticion, whiche any person hathe, or myghte haue in the bread and wyne, it shall suffyse that the bread bee such, as is usuall to bee eaten at the Table with other meates, but the best and purest wheate bread, that conueniently maye be gotten. And yf any of the bread or wine remayne, the Curate shal haue it to hys owne use."

Well, we have come a long way in many areas although it is clear that there are still plenty of questions to be thought out with respect to Eucharistic practice. The question of frequent communion has, in a peculiar way, nullified that fear which Cranmer's second Prayer Book had concerning *superstition*. In fact, I might add that perhaps we could try and take on a little more superstition, meaning devotion and awareness of the Mystery that we approach. Anglo-Catholic oriented people were very happy to see the Eucharist becoming more and more the central liturgical act every Sunday morning, but perhaps by the very frequency of it we may have inadvertently nullified a little of the significance, even while recognizing that this is what the earliest Christians enacted when they met every Sabbath to commemorate the Resurrection.

The Roman Church, although they have always had a Mass centred regimen, suffers from the same problem in this regard as do Anglicans. There was the day when praying the mass weekly but receiving the sacrament only when one had been to confession was the norm. Anglicans used to take receiving communion much more seriously as well. I was talking with a Roman seminarian some years ago and he told me that he felt they were 'over-Eucharistized'. At that time I didn't really appreciate what he was saying as I then believed their situation to be ideal. He was a very wise young man for his years.

Along with the problem of unpreparedness for receiving communion there are a few other elements of worship, which have helped to trivialize the whole experience. Some of those things are the happy-clappy atmosphere that frequently accompanies worship to ostensibly make it more contemporary. There is also the seemingly misguided preference for hymns which lack any real substance or majesty. This trend is common to most churches I think. There are a lot of YouTube clips showing just how trendy and chic a lot of parishes are and they are particularly of interest to (and probably often posted by) the anti-Vatican II crowd as well as for Anglicans who would really prefer their parishes to be Baptist or Pentecostal. Often the impetus behind a lot of this fad is the belief that it will draw in young people, who I believe see straight through it from the outset.

Some other current trends have unfortunately been quite disastrous. One of them is the practice of using ordinary bread for the Eucharist, sometimes even having different people each week baking 'special' altar breads using recipes that are supposedly more like the bread Jesus would have used in the Upper Room to institute the Eucharist.

I was invited some years ago to go to my former college chapel to say Mass. The College had been amalgamated years before and there were only a handful of people at this early celebration—a rather disappointing change from the days when the entire college community of some 30 or 40 people would gather daily. The first time I went a small, round and very dense loaf (cookie) appeared at the time of the offertory. When it came time for the fraction I had considerable difficulty in even breaking it as well as a problem choking it down when I made my communion.

After Mass two women who had assisted joined me in the sacristy to help clear up and to consume any bread that remained. I was appalled that this was done in the midst of much chit-chat, gossiping and giggling. On my second invitation to celebrate there I made sure that I calculated exactly how many communicants there would be and broke the host/loaf into the precise number needed so that there would be nothing remaining. The portions were quite large as I recall and I noticed that they each had surprised expressions on their faces as they chewed and tried to swallow it. Mercifully, I was not invited again.

The other incident which is seared in my memory happened at a synod Eucharist. There were about 350 people at that service. I was seated quite near the front of the church so I was able to see clearly what was happening at the altar and the several communion stations. The first thing that astonished me was when, at the offertory, about six huge loaves of home baked, ordinary, white bread were brought to the celebrant. I thought to myself that this would surely be enough for 5,000.

Soon it was time for the administration. People with chalices and ciboria took their places at five or six stations across the front of the church. Being seated near the front, I received communion early on in the process. Back to my place and an attempt to make my thanksgiving amid such a hustle and bustle. Then I watched as everyone came forward. The station immediately in front of where I was seated was manned (if that is politically correct to say) by a woman who had been an Anglican nun many decades ago, with a ciborium/basket. At one point near the end of distribution I noticed her look down at the floor around her, which was littered with crumbs and large fragments of bread. Her face registered the horror as she stooped to furtively try to gather up some of the larger pieces of the Sacred Body. It was an utter disaster! The Synod was for all intents and purposes over and I made my way hastily to the parking lot and drove home.

Another abuse of the sacrament I believe occurred while I was at St. James' and this was certainly not of our doing. I had never worked in a parish where there were so few problems or conflicts. Things worked like clockwork after more than a century of ministry. The parish was largish, if that is a word, with three masses and Sung Evensong each Sunday. The three priests on staff knew the people for the most part, allowing that we often had visitors who found us in the midst of skid-road and because we had a Solemn High Mass each Sunday.

One Sunday there appeared a young man who we had never seen before—nicely dressed and looking like he might be a university student. When he appeared at the altar rail I placed a host on his extended hands and he immediately rose and departed, without consuming the host—right out of the church. Curious! He appeared again about two months later and the same scenario unfolded. This was noticed by my colleagues and we discussed it afterward. We even wondered if it might have something to do with the occult but were not concerned that the Blessed Sacrament could possibly be inappropriately used for any black purpose. We decided to watch for him in the future. He did appear on a third occasion and this time I indicated discreetly with hand gestures that I would communicate him directly on the tongue, which is what happened. Again, he rose immediately and left the church never to return again to my knowledge.

The theology of Jesus' real presence in the Eucharist certainly must be seen as a positive thing and never in any magical way. It is strength to the believer and never of any use as a negative thing to those who would try and desecrate the sacrament, whatever they might think they are doing with it. Many years ago during a discussion of the real presence in a parish study group, someone asked the question, "But Father, what would happen if at Mass, when the celebrant fractured the priest's host and a part of it flew off and went down behind the altar and couldn't be found?" My colleague answered that impossibly hypothetical question with one of his typically practical remarks, "Well, if He got in there I'm sure He could get out."

✠

Most of the many national Anglican Prayer Books that have been produced over the last three or so centuries have made suggestions in the rubrics of the Order for Holy Communion about bread and wine. Generally, they suggest good quality wheat bread and a suitable wine. Usually in Anglican parishes a port or sherry is the choice. Sometimes there are concerns in dealing with people who might have an alcohol problem or difficulties with gluten. It is often simple enough to suggest receiving only in one species as the church has always taught that Our Lord is fully present in each. But occasionally there is the person who has a gluten problem and also one with alcohol. There have been some provisions made for non-glutinous bread I believe although I never personally encountered that difficulty.

St. James seems to have been in a category of its own with regard to the choice of sacramental wine. For the sixty odd years I was associated with the parish a sacramental Sauterne (white) was used, which supposedly didn't stain linens; this was, at least, the explanation. I have always found that lipstick is more of a problem in that regard than red wine. The use of white wines is undoubtedly more common in Roman churches. In one parish that I served I took it upon myself to buy a gallon of that particular Sauterne from the local Roman church supply house. Upon the very first use of it I received quite a strong objection from a number of people and in particular a choir member who was the commanding officer at the local airforce base. We discussed it a little and his main point seemed to be that red wine symbolizes the precious blood. It had never occurred to me that this was such an important notion, nor that we knew just what sort of wine Jesus and the 12 were drinking at the Last Supper, although it probably was red. Discussion about this objection went on amongst the altar servers and lay readers and some bright person made the flippant comment, "Well, he's perhaps right, you know. We should probably be having red wine with meat anyway." To which another wag quipped, "Following that logic through, we might find a supplier who could provide some streaky bacon hosts!" We always relied on the presumption that Jesus has a sense of humour.

I learned a very practical lesson on one occasion from my friend Father Lloyd Wright, a colleague at St. James'. One evening when he and I were having a quiet dinner in the clergy house after an evening Mass I mentioned to him that something was troubling me a little. I was preparing that year to attend a summer school in Strasbourg sponsored by the local theological college, which had some time ago become ecumenical. I saw in the information brochure that the opening Eucharist would be celebrated by a faculty member who was a Baptist minister, using the then new English *Alternative Service Book*. I explained to Father Wright that I was reluctant to participate in a service with a non-priest celebrating, but that with a group of 45 people, if I avoided the service, or did not communicate it would be glaringly noticed. It was bothering me somewhat because I didn't want to seem to exaggerate the point or open any needless discussion about it. Father Wright pondered this for a moment and then looked at me and in his infinite wisdom said, "Don, I wouldn't concern myself about it. A little piece of bread can't hurt you."

In summing up these thoughts on the Eucharist I want to end with a very brief story. It occurred when a parish family was in their car driving home from a Sunday celebration of High Mass. The younger of their two boys was about six years old at the time. Mother, wanting to talk about what they had just witnessed said to the six year old, "Well, David, did you understand anything of what happened at church today?" "Yes," he responded, without a pause, "I understood all of it!"

Fr. Donald Andrew Dodman

FIVE

FAITH AND WORKS ACCORDING TO SS. PAUL AND JAMES

New Testament III
February 5, 1968

Saint Paul and Saint James at first glance appear to contradict one another concerning the question of justification. Paul says in Romans 3:28 "a man is justified by faith apart from the works of the law," while James, in the second chapter of his epistle (verse 24) says, "You see that a man is justified by works and, not by faith alone". However, even though it appears that these two men were teaching diametrically opposed doctrines, on a closer inspection we find that they are actually in agreement with each other. They each look at the issue from different angles and each one is stressing different facets of the Church's teaching about justification.

One of the first problems in dealing with this question is one that revolves around the word "justify" (δικαιουν). Does it mean to "be counted as righteous" or "to be made righteous"? On an examination of the use of this word in the Septuagint and other references in the Greek New Testament we find that the word always has the meaning "to acquit" or "to pronounce guiltless". It is a forensic term meaning "to freely forgive" as in the case of the Prodigal Son who was forgiven completely and treated with honour without an inquest into his personal attitudes. Some of the references where this word is used are; the Septuagint, 2 Sam 15:4, Isaiah 5:25, Exodus 83:7, Matthew 11:19 and 12:37 Luke 7:55.

Nowhere in Romans does "justify" mean "to make righteous". St. Augustine in an attack against Pelagius says, "all man's holiness is due to the free grace of God". It is true that St. Augustine himself uses the word in both ways, however the theory appears to be that by an infusion of grace by faith men are justified. Men are placed by God in a right relationship with Himself. As soon as we intimate that man's righteousness has any bearing on God's act of forgiveness then we are opening the floodgates to allow the very thing against which St. Paul speaks. This would be making God do precisely what the Prodigal's father did not do—give some place to man's attainment of righteousness as a condition of acceptance. We are justified by and through faith, which is an act of self surrender. The legal flavour of the verb δικαζω implies that there is a judge, the accused and the law—God being the Judge, man being the accused, and for the law the Mosaic law or the Law of Christ. The law of Christ is of course the Law of Faith and love, which man must obey in order to be justified.

Paul uses the words "justification by faith" to describe the radical change that had come into his own life. He had tried to be obedient to the Law (the Torah) and he certainly had succeeded—he was a Hebrew among Hebrews. After his conversion experience he no longer felt that he was condemned but rather justified and acquitted before God. He no longer had to strive after the works of the law but could accept the free gift of grace won for him by Christ. Now the task was to live up to the expectations that went along with the gift of grace. Paul, however, would not admit that the law had been cancelled out by faith. The Law had two meanings: 1) a code of commands and 2) a wider meaning, God's revelation in the Old Testament. This wider conception is what Paul has in mind when he says, "we must uphold the law". Paul's Greek readers would most likely have in their minds only the narrower meaning of "the Law".

Saint James, on the other side of this coin, speaks out in defence of works as opposed to faith. This would appear at first glance to be an attack against Paul's teaching. Martin Luther came to the conclusion that the Epistle of James was not authentic because of the contradiction. He called it an "epistle of straw" and even added the word 'alone' to Paul's Letter to the Romans 3:28, "justified by faith alone".

By works St. James is not implying that our works, related to the Law, are the principal or meritorious cause of our justification. (George Bull, D.D., Harmonia Apostolica, p. 10. The particle "by" [εξ] does not always carry the meaning "cause" [εξ εργων]. It is sometimes used in a lowered sense as in "the manner of obtaining anything". This usage is neither unusual nor strange to the style of scripture. (George Bull, loc. cit.)

To St. James faith meant giving intellectual assent to belief in God. This was not enough as far as he was concerned. One must surely believe intellectually, but one must also manifest his belief in actions. "If Thou believe that God is one; thou doest well, the devils also believe and shudder" (Jas 2:19). On the other hand Paul understood faith to mean "personal adhesion".

Both St. Paul and St. James use the reference to Abraham to support their views. St. Paul sees Abraham as one who through his great faith is justified before God (Gen 15:6). St. James regards Abraham's justification as being affected by his works—the offering up (or rather the intended offering up) of his son Isaac. It is quite evident here that the line of demarcation is very thin.

When Paul speaks of works he has in mind the works of the Law. He is opposing cold Jewish legalism. St. James is rebuking the cold and barren orthodoxy, which is divorced from life when he says that faith alone is not enough--in other words, one must put one's beliefs into action.

Some scholars, including St. Augustine, think that the Epistle of St.

James was written as a warning to those who had mistaken Paul's meaning when he stresses faith above works. On the other hand, another school of thinking dates the Epistle of James to about 50 A.D. and claims that Paul, knowing of the misuse of James 2:14-16 by the Judaisers attempted to correct the misconception.

The Jews had gone to extremes on the side of works (of the Law), then the pendulum swung the other way and many Christians ignored works altogether. James was really reaffirming that works were necessary as well as faith. He looks on works as being proof of faith, not as a means of salvation. Backing up this view we have in Matthew 7:20 "by their fruits ye shall know them" and in Luke 5:8, John the Baptist speaking about "fruits worthy of repentance".

As a reaction against the medieval doctrine of works and in an attempt to exclude all vestige of human merit some have fallen into what is called "solifidianism" or the doctrine of "faith alone".

There seems to be no doubt then, that Paul and James are really of one accord, teaching that both a commitment of the heart and a putting into action of this commitment are necessary in order to be justified by God.

REFLECTIONS ON FAITH AND WORKS
May 2012

Embarrassment would perhaps be the word that leapt to my mind as I looked over this essay on Faith and Works, principally because of its brevity. It might more usefully have been employed as an exam question because although there are a few issues to be dealt with it is not really all that complex, however it did lead me now into new and uncharted thoughts, on which I will elaborate.

Paul and James, as I remarked in the closing paragraph of the essay, were undoubtably of much the same mind, although because of the background of each man the ideas found slightly different nuances of expression. James was undoubtedly thinking that one's *works* were the result of having faith. One behaves toward others with compassion because of belief in a forgiving and loving God, thus good works are ultimately rooted in having faith or perhaps just a sense of moral values. Paul, on the other hand, was understood to be arguing that Christians' good works would not play a role in their salvation but only their faith. Of course, the two things operate in concert. Perhaps Paul might have been wiser to have used the word *grace* instead of faith, because it is surely by God's grace that faith and works are related and function in relation to one another.

Then there is the question of Luther's reaction to the question and his impulse to add the word 'alone' to Paul's (Rom. 3:28) "justified by faith *alone*." That is, of course, the point at which Luther's protestant views are most fully revealed. He was undoubtedly reading from the Latin Vulgate version and was offended by the phrase '*operibus legis*' or 'works of the law' and was reacting to the Medieval abuses of corruption, the sale of indulgences (works again) and God only knows what else. Thus was sparked a whole movement, which undoubtedly was timely, but as is typical with such emotional reactions it was likely stated in an exaggerated fashion. His impetuous personality probably had quite an influence on his actions, but then of course the same is perhaps true for Paul's approach, which we will unravel a little more in due course.

I step back now momentarily to my teenage years when I had become seriously interested in church and was beginning to entertain a little more tangibly the possibility of a career as a priest. Every time I went to Mass I was mildly curious when I heard in the words of the Prayer for the Church, *"Almighty and Everliving God, who by thy holy Apostle hast taught us to make prayers, and supplications, and to give thanks, for all men."* Which holy Apostle? I would think to myself.

For some inexplicable reason I have never quite liked St. Paul and I always thought that surely that reference must be to Peter, Mark, or one of Jesus' close friends. I was familiar enough with the historical framework to know that Paul was a relative latecomer, in spite of the fact that he wrote almost a third of the New Testament.

To set the scene before launching into my thesis, I should explain a few details about how the books of the bible, from the vast collection of documents available in the first few centuries, came to be where they are today in the biblical corpus. During the first three or four centuries of the Christian Era the Church Fathers in council debated this issue for what must have seemed like forever. The various churches (Jerusalem, Antioch, Alexandria and so on) used readings and manuscripts that they had in their possession as well as sharing these precious parchments amongst their various communities. There were many Gospels, letters and writings to choose from including the ones we are familiar with in the canon of scripture.

Some of those other ones, like the gospels of Thomas, Judas, Philip, Nicodemus and others perhaps number somewhere around thirty. Over the course of time consensus was somehow achieved and we have the three Synoptic Gospels and the Gospel of St. John, which appear in the present New Testament collection. It is truly amazing to me that, save for a very few exceptions, all Christians agree on what is contained in a mutually accepted canon of scripture.

A few of the exceptions are the books of the Apocrypha, or Intertestamental Writings, which Roman Catholics accept as fully scriptural books, while Anglicans use these readings for *edification but not doctrine,* and they are included in the Anglican daily office lectionary. Protestants completely reject them. Interestingly, the Revelation of St. John the Divine is not used for readings in the Greek Church but all other Orthodox bodies do accept it as canonical. The Apocalypse of John is very esoteric and cryptic as he was writing under the eyes of the Roman empire and by necessity had to use imagery that would escape notice except for the initiated who would certainly understand who, for instance, the Whore of Babylon was.

Many Christians adore the Book of Revelation because is it a gold mine of potentially crazy ideas, if one is so inclined, and one can make the most outrageous and reckless interpretations.

Personally, I feel that it would have been better if they had omitted it from the canon entirely, simply because of the confusion that it could engender. During the councils and debates dealing with the canon, St. John's Gospel was thought to have been in a bit of a precarious position, although it was finally included. Part of the reason for its inclusion was undoubtedly because of John's close relationship with Mary, Jesus Mother. John's Revelation is considered to be an apocalyptic writing of tremendous imagination, imagery and wealth if used acknowledging what it is, but naturally fundamentalists and those who lack a sense of the poetic insist on believing it to be literal. I believe it would have been so much more edifying to have included the beautiful, pastoral and sane Letter of Clement in its place.

But, to get past that introduction to my point, there are reasons why I seriously question why Paul's writing gained such prominence. Before delving into details, I should mention that during those years of debate and consultation about the canon there was one man, a priest of a city in what is now Turkey, who had a revolutionary idea about what the Christian canon should contain. His name was Marcion of Sinope, a priest and theologian. He was eventually branded a heretic for his radical ideas and after reading what is to follow here, I might easily be accorded that same distinction.

Marcion was chiefly remarkable because he was convinced that the Christian canon should completely omit the Old Testament. The majority of people believed that the Old Testament was important because it foreshadowed the coming of a Messiah and that it undergirded the basis of the New Testament. I think that so many of the Church's problems today are exacerbated by dragging the Old Covenant into the debate— particularly the Holiness Code of Leviticus, which for Christians is in any case actually irrelevant. And I am adamant in asserting that no living person could possibly comply with every detail of the bible in reality. Those who like it seem to like little bits of it that underscore their favourite notions while completely ignoring the more absurd and ridiculous restrictions in it. They would do well to read it in its entirety to understand what they are actually espousing. I am sure, however, that the Latter Prophets would be no problem. Isaiah, Jeremiah, Micah and the likes of Joel, who represent a much more developed spiritual understanding of God and the world, would most certainly present little difficulty. They would surely be seen as quite in harmony with the teachings and attitudes of Jesus. In fact most of the Latter Prophets indeed did tend to contribute to the shaping and moulding of Jesus' teaching and attitudes

Now, back to Paul of Tarsus. I find that I even have difficulty referring to him as *Saint* Paul. What I am going to attempt to do is audacious really, because I am no biblical scholar, and I do not wish to draw this out in detail which would surely require another book as it is an immensely complex issue. Allow me to formulate my thoughts in a more general way—perhaps as questions and issues that have vexed me for decades and perhaps intersperse those questions with the occasional observation based on my reading and thinking over these forty-five years.

First, to give Paul his due and to set the scene, I should begin by acknowledging that Paul's writing contains much of value for the Christian Church in its teaching capacity. We need also to notice that there is a rather unique relationship between the undisputed seven letters of Paul and the Acts of the Apostles. The undisputed seven letters are: Romans, First and Second Corinthians, Galatians, Philippians, First Thessalonians and the letter to Philemon. The others, often attributed to Paul, are held by most enlightened scholars to have been written by individuals who were possibly associates or even just sympathizers with the school of Paul. This sort of emulation and practise was not at all unusual with respect to documents of antiquity.

The other important thing to point out is that Luke, or perhaps a follower of Luke, is by many believed to be the writer of the Acts of the Apostles since as early as the 2nd Century. One cannot help but sense that this writer was a supporter, devotee or even possibly an advocate for Paul.

My questions and doubts about Paul are partially rooted in the fact that Paul's writings appeared on the scene some ten years before any of the four canonical Gospel accounts were written. This means, curiously, that the authors of the four Gospels could well have had access to Paul's writing and conversely that Paul did *not* have access to those Gospels while he was writing. This may explain, at least in part, some of the angst I feel about Paul. I would even conjecture that if the New Testament canon had been organized in order of its historical composition we might not now be experiencing some of the problems we are facing, but of course scholarship in this arena is for the most part relatively recent.

Now, let us examine some of the curious notions that spring to my mind about the Blessed Apostle. First of all, Paul boasted that he was a Jew, not only a Pharisee but a Hebrew among Hebrews of the tribe of Benjamin, and yet it is very well documented that his knowledge of the Hebrew scriptures comes always from his familiarity with the Septuagint—the Greek version of the Hebrew Bible, which actually is not unusual for Jews of the Diaspora (those scattered around the Middle East.) Paul claims that he was born in Tarsus in Asia Minor, which was without a doubt a Hellenistic enclave where there would have been probably a small Jewish community.

Then he claims that he went to Jerusalem to live and study. He never seems to offer any details about whether his family moved there when he was very young, or perhaps if he moved on his own in his late teens or early twenties. He curiously rarely mentions parents or siblings, which I find quite odd, especially for one who seems often to freely reveal many other facets of his personal life.

He lives in Jerusalem, according to what we read in the Acts of the Apostles, at about the time that Jesus would have been much in the news, yet Paul never makes mention of this, even though it must have been the talk of the town—especially Jesus' trial and crucifixion. Indeed, Paul it appears never actually met Jesus in the flesh, or at least he does not mention it, which is also curious.

Paul later on claims to have become a persecutor of the Christian Church, supposedly as an official sanctioned by the High Priest. Remember now, that Paul was a Pharisee—a sect of the most zealous group within Judaism. The High Priest, however, at that time happened to be a Sadducee, typically representing more moderate views. Paul, apparently under the aegis of the High Priest, set out to begin his persecution of the

Church, and not in Jerusalem but in Damascus, Syria—not a part of the Jewish world in any sense—to deal with followers of this Nazarene and on his way has a dramatic encounter with a vision of Jesus. Mention of this event appears only in the account of Paul's life in the Acts of the Apostles, save for a somewhat obscure reference in the First Letter to the Corinthians, *"And last of all he was seen of me also, as one born out of due time"*. *This reference is a curiosity because of its vagueness as Paul's tendency seems normally to over dramatize and adorn with considerable detail.*

In his letters Paul never alludes to any of the sayings, teachings or attitudes of Jesus, which is odd because he would certainly have been in contact with numerous communities of Christians and have been well aware of the tradition. It seems that the only time Paul allows himself to become involved with the life of Jesus is a section in First Corinthians which speaks of Jesus' Passion, Crucifixion and Resurrection. This is the only time when the Jesus tradition is drawn into the picture. Paul recounts the institution of the Lord's Supper and one assumes that this recollection does come down to him by way of the tradition of the Church, perhaps through the ever-elusive Luke.

This situation is surely because his only contact with Christ is from his own visions and dreams, which no one else shared. Paul has, I believe, fabricated and shaped the very system which he has single-handedly directed. My first impulse is to imagine that perhaps Paul was the victim of some sort of personal or mental affliction. We know so much more now about bipolar disorders and schizophrenia and how common such things can be.

He speaks also about being besieged by a 'thorn in the flesh', which he pleads with God to remove but which He does not. Paul says that God responds to him in this way, *"My grace is sufficient for thee: for my strength is made perfect in weakness".* Whatever it was is one of the greatest mysteries concerning Paul—and many have wondered whether it might possibly have been failing eyesight or perhaps some sort of illness. Some have also expressed the thought that maybe Paul was gay, but that is quite possibly transposing our own thoughts and presumptions into the mix, however plausible it may be. There are times when Paul does sound somewhat self-loathing and sensitive about himself.

On some occasions Paul inserts peculiar and seemingly inappropriate opinions. For instance in I Corinthians chapter 11 when he is explaining how he understands the relationship between men and women the narrative seems to read like Paul's stream of consciousness. As he drifts randomly from one thought to the next in the course of this, he interjects thoughts about how long hair is a shame for a man but a glory for a woman without giving any rational explanation.

Perhaps his fixation with hair is somehow related to the fact that he was going bald and might have been bothered about it. There are moments when it doesn't even sound like Paul writing, particularly when he goes on about women being submissive to their husbands and keeping silent during worship, which seems even to contradict other opinions he held about equality; "there is neither Jew nor Greek, slave nor free, male nor female". A few scholars have conjectured that possibly texts handed down to us had even been corrupted by copyists adding bits and pieces of rather incongruous and incompatible material much like what happened with the spurious ending of Mark's Gospel.

Issues like these simply tend to magnify the complexity of our faith, in my opinion and lead inevitably to questions regarding who actually did found Christianity. Jesus himself, in the Gospel accounts, did not seem to be inclined to found any structured institution—in fact, quite the contrary.

In Paul's letters he strangely almost never uses the name Jesus alone. It seems that he harboured some kind of conflict between the man Jesus and the title the *Christ*. I realize from experience that some Christians seem to believe that Jesus was his first name and Christ was his second or family name rather than Christ being a title. Paul does not seem to relate to the humanness of Jesus in a very explicit way, perhaps because he had never actually encountered Jesus in the flesh. This is perhaps one of the reasons why fundamentalists seem to be so fond of Paul, and especially Romans because for Paul, human nature is unfortunately so profoundly afflicted with sin and fallenness.

Somehow this also seems to be linked intimately with Paul's theology of the atonement in which God substitutes his Son for humanity and allows Him to die to save mankind. This view is technically called *penal substitution*. It is extrapolated from Paul's thinking and is associated most often with Reformation theology and of course, Paul's Letter to the Romans. That God demanded a victim to atone for the sins of men is one of the central doctrines of fundamentalists and is perhaps why they tend to focus on that aspect while minimizing the inclusive, loving and forgiving attitudes of Jesus which are so evident in the Gospels. Substitutionary atonement is, of course, closely tied up with the notion of original sin, which in any case has little scriptural basis.

In Christian theology the atonement refers to the forgiving or pardoning of sin through the death of Jesus Christ, which made possible the reconciliation between God and creation. Within the purview of Christian doctrine there are, historically four or five theories for how such atonement might be explained: the ransom theory, sometimes called the *Christus Victor* model, the satisfaction theory, the penal substitution theory and the moral influence model.

Penal substitution obviously is the approach that Paul prefers, although granted, he does not actually use those precise words and in any case the other theories were not even propounded until many centuries after Paul's time. However, Paul's argument is that Christ, by his own sacrificial choice, was punished (penalized) in the place of sinners, thus satisfying the demands of justice so that God is able to forgive man's sins.

I confess that I am not quite sure what I'm trying to achieve in spelling all of this out. I fully realize that it would never be possible to alter the biblical canon at this late date as it has been so universally accepted by the churches and by some even deified. To remove Paul from it would be impossible, even though my suspicion is that he has distorted and refashioned Jesus far beyond recognition.

For some odd reason many Christians seem to be obsessed with questions about sexuality, and one wonders just how much Paul has been responsible for promoting that trend. With regard specifically to questions of sexual ethics and attitudes towards women, it is somehow shocking that almost all of the biblical texts one hears bandied about seem to be either from Leviticus or the letters of Paul.

Occasionally I fantasize in my wildest dreams and wonder just where Jesus stands on the behaviour of many Christians and church bodies. Thoughts in this vein also bring back to my memory a comment made by Ghandi on an occasion when he was asked his opinion of Christianity. He apparently said, *"Well, I like your Christ, but I don't like your Christians. Your Christians are so unlike your Christ"*. I confess that I do have moments of despair on occasion. In any case it does cause one to ponder about just how Christianity was shaped and transmitted to us.

SIX

CLERICAL CELIBACY
Moral Theology III
November 15, 1967

Clerical Celibacy has never really been particularly highly regarded especially in Anglican and Non-Conformist circles. It has been seen as a denial of earthly pleasures and a renunciation of the world. St. Jerome and others have attempted to encourage celibacy although even he admitted that it was not practical in the early church. Saint Thomas Aquinas himself claimed that Christ would not have forced Peter to leave his wife in order to minister in the Church. There is a decided leaning toward the celibate state in the theology of St. Paul and it is probably because he believed that the Parousia, or the end of time, was very near.

EARLY INTEREST IN ASCETICISM

Early in the history of the Christian Church men began to entertain ideas that the highest possible service to God could better be rendered when the soul was free from the passions, which are part of normal human functions. It was commonly held that sexual commerce would taint the soul. Hence we have examples at this time of self mutilation. Origen is the name that immediately flashes to most people's minds in this respect. He later condemned the practical rendering of the text on which this was based (Matthew 19:12) but alas it was too late! The text is, of course, the one where Jesus says if the eye offend you, pluck it out. Origen, as a normal man with sexual impulses, took the text literally and castrated himself hoping to end his lustful desires and remain chaste and celibate. Priests were often deposed if their wives were taken in adultery because it was believed that this had tainted their priestly office.

In 305 AD it was formally acknowledged by the Council of Elvira that the husband of a second wife was not to be admitted to Holy Orders. Hippolytus,

Bishop of Portus, in the third century writes a criticism against Pope Calixtus accusing him of admitting men to Orders who had been married twice or more, and for allowing men already in orders to become married. The Council of Nicea did not make any legislation in regard to the marriage of the clergy, as it did not seem to have been much of an issue at that particular time. The practise of celibacy seems to have been formally introduced into the Latin Church about 384 and from that time it spread gradually over the whole of the Western Church.

In England celibacy was introduced to the Saxons in 597 by St. Augustine, but it was not well received. Augustine found it so difficult to find coworkers because of the celibacy rule that he appealed to Pope Gregory to ask for permission to allow those who could not possibly abide the rule to marry but remain active in the ministry. Gregory answered very evasively outlining what Augustine already understood—that those in lower orders (lower than deacons) could marry if they so desired. He purposely omitted saying anything about the higher orders of clergy. "He apparently did not wish to assume the responsibility of relaxing the rule, while willing perhaps to connive at its suspension in order to encourage the infant Anglican Church." (H. C. Lea, The History of Sacerdotal Celibacy in the Christian Church, p. 129). It appears that for a period of time the discipline of the Church was reasonably maintained. From the 9th to the 11th centuries there was increasing neglect, which is well documented, in a detailed history of councils and decrees.

Clergy were not the only people to submit themselves to the rule of celibacy in this age. From about 1120 to 1167 we see the rise of the Military Orders, the Knights of which submitted themselves to the celibate life. This was a strange mixture of military and religious enthusiasm. These people were involved in the Crusades and other religiously motivated programmes. The Hospitallers (Knights of St. John of Jerusalem), a group of men interested in treating the wounded, could easily give up their humble position and assume military duties. Their order required that they take the three ordinary monastic vows of poverty, obedience and chastity. This group was in the beginning associated with the Benedictine order.

There is a period from the thirteenth century to the fifteenth century when heresies crept in and in which a considerable amount of perversion of the celibate life abounded. With the coming of the Reformation in Germany there was a breakdown in the area of traditional thought. With this came a great deal of thinking and rethinking of the place of the celibate life. We find the first example of sacerdotal marriage connected with Luther in 1521. He himself married in 1525. From this time onward in Germany the monastic ideal and interest in the celibate priesthood (among Protestants) began to dissolve.

In the Anglican Church, in spite of the fact that a break with Rome had occurred, celibacy was still the norm. Henry VIII was actually one of the great defenders of the celibate priesthood. There are records of persecutions of married priests dating from the year 1539. We do find however, an interest in priestly marriage beginning to appear around 1563. Throughout history there has been an interest in priestly marriage among French churchmen—even since the Reformation and continuing until the present day. One example of a modern change toward a view of the married priesthood is the position of the Old Catholic Church, which gave up the idea of a compulsory celibacy when they broke with the Roman Church in 1878.

THE THEOLOGY OF THE CELIBATE LIFE

As we have already stated above, St. Paul was rather reluctant to fully sanction the married state. He felt that it was better to remain single (celibate) but that if one could not do this it was better that he marry. "I wish that all were as I myself am." (I Corinthians 7:7). Paul felt that he could give himself more completely to God if he did not have other demanding responsibilities.

Max Thurian in his book <u>Marriage and Celibacy</u> makes a point which is crucial in any discussion of the celibate life, which is that marriage and celibacy must both be considered together—they are both vocations and some men and women are called to one or the other of these vocations. In other words celibacy is not simply the state of a man or woman who has not had the opportunity of marriage. One, in order to be celibate in the true sense, chooses this type of life and takes on the responsibilities involved just as in marriage one takes on certain responsibilities.

THE SACRIFICE OF CELIBACY

Thurian feels that Jesus' life presents us with a valid foundation for celibacy. He feels that the celibate state is a sign of the absolute demands of Christ and of the fervent desire of the Church for Jesus' return. "If any man will come after me let him deny himself and take up his cross and follow me, for whoever will lose his life for my sake shall find it." (Matt. 10:38) One who espouses celibacy is not to become less human; he is to open his life to the fullness of Christ and to come to know life more fully.

Jesus was no less human because he had no other love than that of his brothers and no other bride than the Church. In undertaking the celibate life one is actually renouncing the old order of creation for the new order of the Kingdom of Heaven. In the New Testament we read often of those "who made themselves eunuchs for the kingdom of God". This is not necessarily meant to be taken literally but rather as a spiritual concept—they remained unmarried in order to be of more service to God.

VOLUNTARY CELIBACY

Jesus speaks of eunuchs who are in that state because of their birth or by accident. This concept of celibacy could certainly be called into question. The type of celibacy that we are dealing with is actually a state entered upon with complete knowledge and acceptance—as one would enter into a marriage. It requires a particular gift of God. In other words it involves a life long commitment, not just a state where one waits patiently to discover whether or not the opportunity of marriage comes along. The celibate person has made a choice.

In the early Church there was a decided notion that the celibate state was more preferable than the married state. One must be careful not to fall into an exaggerated position on either side of the issue. The idea that marriage was a lesser state was probably engendered by the low level of moral conduct in the Greco-Roman world. Early Christians were most likely somewhat reactionary in this regard.

THE VALUE OF CELIBACY TO THE CHURCH

There is a certain practical usefulness that an unmarried priest can offer to the disposal of the Church. He is able to go virtually anywhere and to work under any conditions, which he would not be able to do if he had the responsibilities of marriage. He is unattached (to a great degree) to the things of the world and can consequently give wholly of himself to the service of the Church.

In the Diocese of Caledonia at the present time there are approximately five Indian villages where it is not really feasible to send a married priest. The Bishop can really only engage men who are celibate. The married priest must be concerned with the health of his family (even if this means a wife only), the education of his children and a multitude of other considerations. One cannot neglect one's family for God and consequently we must have men who are prepared to work in areas with adverse conditions. However, at the same time we must be honest and admit that there are instances where marriage is preferable to celibacy. Paul foresaw that there would be persecutions (and martyrdoms) and because of this he argued for celibacy. (1 Corinthians 7:28)

The celibate priest is able to give himself completely to mankind. This is also useful when one considers the situation where people require extended and prolonged help. A priest who is a confessor also has an advantage if he is celibate, because he does not have the temptation to share his burdens with his wife, with whom he would presumably be intimate.

It is sometimes claimed that an unmarried priest cannot possibly counsel married people. This is, of course nonsense. A priest no more has to be married to counsel married people than he has to be neurotic to counsel neurotic people. The Holy Spirit guides men in ministering to other souls. The celibate priest experiences spiritual fatherhood.

There is also another aspect of the celibate life that can become extremely central in the life and work of a priest. This is the life of devotion. One can cultivate a special relationship with Christ through prayer and contemplation. Paul speaks of being "holy in body and spirit". (I Corinthians 7:34)

The monastic ideal of course fits into this framework. One can be wholly consecrated to the service of Christ in body and spirit. Thurian also, in <u>Marriage and Celibacy</u>, speaks of "pleasing God with the whole of one's being". The life of Mary, the Mother of our lord, is an example of the complete and utter devotion to and dependence upon God. The celibate life can be lonely but we are promised by our Lord that when we give up brothers, sisters, and family we will be recompensed a hundredfold.

THEOLOGICAL SIGNIFICANCE

In one sense the celibate life is a sign of the order where we are neither given nor taken in marriage. Because of this it can be said to have eschatological significance. It implies that we should not put too much faith in the things of this world. As has been mentioned before, it is also a sign of the coming of the Kingdom.

One point which is certainly important in any discussion of this subject is the idea that E. G. Knipp-Fisher expresses in his article on <u>Celibacy</u>. He feels that celibacy must be grounded in theology. No matter what the need, the cry for more celibate priests is not very convincing unless we think of it in terms of theology. He also believes that celibacy is a vocation for men, not as Fr. Talbot used often to say "a vocation for the undersexed". It is not a second best but a life of fulfillment.

SOME MODERN TRENDS

In recent years there has been a great deal of material written on the subject of the married and the celibate priesthood most of which has been prompted by the renewal in the Roman Catholic Church. E. G. Knapp-Fisher, <u>Celibacy,</u> p. 149. There have been surveys conducted and polls taken to try and discern what the feeling of the clergy might be on the matter. These attempts usually indicate that many clergy would in fact like to be able to marry or at least they feel that they should have a choice.

In the Anglican Communion we do not have the same problem, however, our problem appears to be at the other end of the continuum—the almost blatant notion that people expect the almost compulsory marriage of the clergy. We need to examine our theology and attitudes toward the celibate life somewhat more carefully. To many people the word 'celibate' is a dirty word. Undoubtedly there will be many changes in thinking in the years to come on all fronts.

BIBLIOGRAPHY:

The Catholic Encyclopedia

Hardy, E.R., Priestly Ministry in the Modern Church

Knapp-Fisher, E. J., Celibacy, (Theology, Vol. 60, 1957, PP. 144-150)

Lea, H. C., A History of Sacerdotal Celibacy in the Christian Church, Russell and Russell, New York, 1957

Niebhur and Williams, The Ministry in Historical Perspective.

Thurian, Max. Marriage and Celibacy

REFLECTIONS ON CLERICAL CELIBACY
JUNE 2012

Perusing this paper now causes me to ask questions of myself which I simply cannot answer because of the passage of time. For instance, why was an essay on the subject even important for an Anglican seminarian? Also, why was the paper included in a moral theology course rather than in a church history context? Is it possible that I perhaps had some choice of subjects and got myself into doing it?   That may have been the reason, as you will possibly guess as I unpack some thoughts about the subject of celibacy.

In order to set things into some sort of context, I should begin by explaining some of the facts which lay behind the scenes. First of all, my professor for this Moral Theology course was Father Richard Mugford who had himself graduated from the Anglican Theological College where all of this drama took place. He was a bachelor priest and a rather eccentric person. He may have actually taken some sort of vow of celibacy for all I know, as some Anglican priests do when they become oblates of certain religious orders. Some years after I graduated, Father Mugford left academia and was received into the Roman Catholic Church. He taught Latin and English at the Seminary of Christ the King at Westminster Abbey near Mission, B.C. for a few years during his formation period and was eventually ordained there. He then became involved in a teaching position with the Education Department of the Archdiocese of Vancouver.

Back for a moment to the original essay. At the end of it I have appended the bibliography of reading material, which I now notice is almost entirely by Roman Catholic authors. I'm sure that was no accident, as Father Mugford knew full well of my interest in the catholic aspects of the Church, aside from the fact that there is a paucity of Anglican material on the subject, except for literature which was directly related to Anglican religious communities where celibacy has always been an integral part of the scheme of things.

It is quite possible that I did have some involvement in the choice of subjects in this case as I was still single at the age of 27 and probably did think that I would be, by default, a celibate priest as I was by then resigned to the fact that I was gay. I recall on a number of occasions when people would refer to me as a celibate priest that I would remind them that I was not celibate—never having taken a vow—but was simply a bachelor. My sexuality was certainly not public knowledge at that time, although I did believe that my life would necessarily be solitary.

This situation in itself probably determined my path to some measure as I spent years living in isolated places—mostly on Indian Reserves—and living in sometimes less than adequate housing. At that time this was no problem for me as I was enthusiastic about being a priest and having work to attend to. It was probably beneficial at that time not to have other responsibilities to concern me. I was free and happy to go to the Arctic part of Québec or to isolated places on the British Columbia Coast and concentrate on the work.

During those periods of isolation I recall two particular instances when I was thankful to be a single entity without having to worry about a wife or children. One incident happened at a time of particular turmoil after I had spoken out rather strongly and publicly about the election of a chief. The current one was doing some very questionable things in dealing with government money and in the management of the Band and, without using any names, I was suggesting that there needed to be change. This divided the community I suppose and caused difficulties, the full details of which I was quite unaware. In any case, before I knew it every window in the church was smashed and I feared for what might happen to the rectory which was not on the reserve but in the centre of the nearby town. However, after the election finally took place they did the right thing, which I thought made it all worthwhile.

The other situation happened in another place, far across the country. Drug trafficking and substance abuse problems became very critical in this isolated community and led to the sad suicide of a young man of the parish. At his funeral the entire village turned out as usual, and filled the small church and most of the churchyard. I knew who some of the drug dealers were and they were right there sitting in the front pews—one even acting as a pallbearer. It was not often that I had the ears of almost the entire community. I spoke softly and in a slow and measured way to an attentive congregation—one could hear a pin drop. I outlined in stark detail just what effect drugs were having on our community. This happened to be the third suicide in several months and the ache spilled over into many of the families. The village was divided, but as is often the case, no one would dare talk about it, which is not unusual in closely-knit communities. I noticed in the weeks following that some people, when passing me on the street, would nod and silently smile, but say nothing. Others would simply look at me with daggers in their eyes and walk on.

Again, I fretted for months worrying that the rectory or the church might be torched. However, mercifully nothing happened! Before many months the Royal Canadian Mounted Police initiated a huge raid and the source of the drugs and the method of shipment was curtailed.

☨

I have often thought of Alexander Pope's writing about clerical celibacy and how a Priest, undistracted by wife and family, can tend to the flock more fully and maintain the confidentiality between himself and his people. It does sound altruistic and noble but I am not quite so sure I really believe it.

I have known married clergy whose wives have been extremely aware of the relationship that their spouses need in order to do their work, knowing just when to disappear and leave people to talk and keeping the marriage and church work in totally separate compartments.

On the other hand, I have known marriages that have been destructive of any pastoral responsibility, where the wife (I should now in this climate be saying spouse, I'm sure) interferes in things that should never be trespassed. There is surely no foolproof way of getting around it. To be logical, if a spouse can diminish the work of a priest and put restrictions on his time, then why can't that also be true for a heart surgeon, a police officer, or a counsellor?

✠

My current interest with regard to the question of celibacy lies especially with the situation in the Roman Catholic Church, which is about the only Church in Christendom insisting upon a celibate priesthood. There would probably be few who had not heard during the past ten years of the scandalous abuses that have plagued the Roman Church, and to be honest which have also affected other church bodies as well.

Discussions and opinions on the subject appear in newspapers and on television almost on a daily basis. The pros and cons about just how celibacy figures into the mix are varied and enormous, however the depth of the problem in the Roman Church is not where my thoughts are leading me at the moment. Naturally, the problem of men and women striving to live celibate and holy lives yet, at the same time trying to suppress natural urges and desires must be monumental for them. I am not sure what effect the celibate life has on people with regard to the cause of the offences that occur. Perhaps in most cases, I should think, the inclination was already there in the beginning. I have to confess that my own vocation to the priesthood in the Anglican Church was probably slightly influenced by my sexuality. After all, it would be easy to explain away the unmarried state as "devoting oneself to God" even though it was never a requirement in the Anglican Church.

There is a hilarious anecdote contained in John Loughery's history of gay life in the 20th century, *The Other Side of Silence*, in which he attests to this quirky attitude. It refers to an incident when Francis Cardinal Spellman of New York was asked about his rather cavalier attitude to his homosexuality. He apparently had a penchant for chorus boys from Broadway in the 1940s, and on one occasion the Prelate, who was known to his friends as "Franny", was driving back to his residence with a young dancer friend. The young man was a little amazed at Spellman's recklessness and asked His Eminence why he wasn't more careful, to which Spellman answered, "Oh, who would ever believe *that*?" How a few decades have changed that point of view!

This approach has unfortunately contributed to the attitude, which appears to have become standard in the upper echelons of the Vatican and is perhaps why they just don't seem able to take it seriously.

It continually amazes me how after all the many incidents and widespread news about abuse the matter seems to have made little dent in or at least an improvement in the situation. A headline this morning on my internet news page asks, WHY, AFTER TEN YEARS HAS THERE BEEN NO CHANGE? Of course, the shame of coverup cuts very deeply. Protect the honour of Mother Church at all costs.

Just move a problem priest, or put him on leave, but don't go to the police, let the Church deal with her own by simply moving them around. I know personally of so many such situations, and yet I still find it appalling that the old ways persist.

The problem of course is really at the very top in the Vatican. The Pope, when he was in charge of the Congregation of the Doctrine of the Faith, even wrote a letter to all Catholic bishops instructing them to contact him personally about such problems and NOT to go to the police or to go public. And the communication even gave explicit instructions that the letter must be kept locked in a safe. The letter was leaked by someone—a bishop presumably—and its contents are to be found all over the internet, and as we all know, when something gets onto the internet it remains there forever. But, it has never to my knowledge been dealt with nor the Vatican called to account. Of course, what good would that do, I suppose.

I haven't really worn a clerical collar for fifteen years now, since my retirement, except on a few occasions. There once was the day when as I walked along the street I was met by smiles and adoring greetings but now it frequently evokes looks of disgust. How things have changed in the past few decades.

There is, of course, more to the rule of celibacy for the Church to deal with than simply the problem of child abuse. First and foremost there is the dreadful lack of priests—especially in north America. Permitting priests to marry would undoubtedly have a profound effect on that decline. Those who are comfortable with, and prefer the celibate life, would hardly be affected. I believe I remarked somewhere in that old college essay about how in the Anglican Communion there used to be an unwritten attitude that there is almost a situation of compulsory marriage. For many parishes it boils down to the notion of getting two for one salary. I believe that I missed out on several parish opportunities because I was single, but of course, that was never actually articulated.

The mention of salary would certainly be my second concern about married clergy in the Roman Church. It would obviously be a radical upset financially for parishes and dioceses, because it would throw the system into chaos. Roman parish priests, if I can make a generalization, make an apparently minimal monthly allowance, which seems to work reasonably well as accommodation, cars, house keepers, groceries, insurance and a multitude of other benefits are provided by either the parish or the diocese, whereas Anglican clerics receive a reasonable stipend, from which the priest looks after all of his or her own amenities and is independent. The stipends that I made were without a doubt lower than those in other professions with a comparable degree of scholarity and experience, however over the course of my career, including the retirement years on my pension, I have managed to travel to Europe and other places fifteen or twenty times for vacation. But, to make such a change now—after a thousand or so years—would certainly be quite a tricky dilemma for Rome.

✠

Not long ago, as I was researching material pertinent to clerical celibacy, I came across information about a retired Australian Catholic bishop who is certainly the first one I have ever heard about who was courageous enough to speak out about a number of the issues that are currently plaguing the church. He is Bishop Geoffrey Robinson, formerly of the Roman Catholic Diocese of Sydney. There are some interesting YouTube interviews with Bishop Robinson, which are well worth visiting.

In a recently published book, *Confronting Power and Sex in the Catholic Church*, Robinson draws out what he believes to be some of the core problems relating to the sexual abuse scandal which for ten or more years has dogged the church. It is obvious from the book's title that he thinks that power is as much related to the problem as sexual behaviour and he is, in a sense, pleading for open and honest discussion in spite of how difficult and painful that would be.

A major part of Bishop Robinson's criticism of the Church's lack of the ability to approach the issue lies right in the Vatican. Given that the church has always professed that Christ has endowed the church with His authority, yet there remains a very tricky problem. That authority rests in the Church's Magisterium or teaching authority, which in effect is all the collected papal decisions down through the centuries. It involves the very nature of tradition and the inspiration of

Holy Scripture as well as the Creeds and the infallibility of Councils and the Popes.

Bishop Robinson's plea for openness and discussion about issues like celibacy and contraception raises many red flags for the Curia and the Vatican. It would mean that the church would inevitably have to say, "Yes, in the past we have made some mistakes which need to be rectified", and that would lead directly to the question of infallibility, which no one dares to even dream of approaching. Unfortunately, it is an absolutist system, which only permits more to be added, but never anything subtracted. The Vatican is in an impossible situation, which probably can never be rectified, at least without a great deal of pain, difficulty and honesty. It is virtually at the breaking point in many respects.

Hans Küng, in his book <u>Disputed Truth (Memoirs II),</u> talks about how very troubled Paul VI was a few years after Vatican II was over because he would not consider approaching the issue of contraception even though it was well known that most Catholics used it and had no problem with it. He knew that he was very unpopular and that his pontificate would be forever tainted because of his inability to confront reality. He was also completely aware that to say anything about contraception, except to forbid it, would mean he was undermining the Doctrine of Infallibility. His encyclical *HUMANAE VITAE* went ahead, the door was now closed for him, and it became yet another problem sealed in the invulnerable Magisterium.

There is a very funny story, in all probability apocryphal, related to this issue. In 1966 Michael Ramsey, Archbishop of Canterbury, visited Paul VI, which was the first time the heads of the Roman Catholic and Anglican Churches had met in 400 years. They met in the Sistine Chapel and signed together a common declaration stressing their desire to work together on issues of mutual importance such as dealing with mixed marriages between Anglicans and Catholics. Michael Ramsey was well known for his impish sense of humour. When it came time to sign the document, Paul VI was first to go. He was given the black fountain pen. He removed the cap and attempted to sign, but it seemed dry. He shook the pen a little, tried again and then looked rather sheepishly at Michael Cantuar, who smiled graciously and said, "Well, no one's infallible". Paul didn't seem get it, one would presume, and I'm sure it wasn't meant maliciously in any case.

Someone then quickly produced another pen and the signing continued.

✠

With respect to my Priesthood and life in general, I have been richly blessed. In spite of wrestling with my own problems in life, and especially with coming to grips with my sexuality, I have been able to have a busy and productive career, which was basically unfettered by personal grief or loneliness. There were the moments of loneliness occasionally, but not threateningly debilitating. The last ten years of my working life were blessed by being in a clergy team with two other priests in a busy inner-city parish. The meals, worship and companionship were wonderfully strengthening and outright fun.

I have been retired now for 15 years—as of yesterday actually. The most amazing thing happened to me shortly after retiring. I thought I was going to slip away quietly into a life of reading, listing to my music tapes, watching movies and doing nothing much of anything. But, out of the blue, I met my significant other—a fabulous young man from Virginia—and we have been married now for ten years. The timing was extremely convenient because I don't believe this would have worked at all when I was engaged in parish work. It is a long story, and far too extended to enter into here—however, in my autobiography, "*A Priest's Tale*" there is a much more detailed treatment of it.

SEVEN

THE OXFORD MOVEMENT
Church History III
March 31, 1967

Most movements throughout history have come as a result of the gradual build up of tension or strong feeling over a long period of time. Usually one cannot pinpoint the exact beginning with any degree of accuracy. The Oxford Movement is one such trend. However, there comes a time when someone finally makes a positive move and initiates what could be called a beginning. Just such a move was made in July of 1833 when John Keble preached his famous Assize Sermon on "National Apostasy" in St. Mary's University Church Oxford.

The Oxford Movement, as it would come to be known, had been formally initiated. Keble and the other Oxford reformers were concerned about the way the Church and the State were so closely bound together; concerned about the interference of the government in the Irish dioceses; disturbed about the degenerate state of the teaching of the Church and desirous of reform in many areas. Keble felt that the "apostolical church" of the land was being betrayed. Because of the close tie between church and state, every person in the country was in a sense a member of the church. He accused the state of "Erastianism"—a Calvinist political theory about absolute state primacy over the church. Whether the accusation was really valid or not is a matter of speculation. There was a terribly large question in his mind over the matter of Prayer Book revision and its dependence on the approval of the state rather than solely on the Church. Keble could not tolerate the management of the Church being handled like a department of the state, as was the case in the trouble over ten Irish Bishoprics.

The problems that arose from the church state relationship were not the only ones that were thorns-in-the-flesh to the Oxford Reformers. There was very often an exceedingly low view of the historic episcopate even amongst the Bishops of the Church. There was a great need for rethinking and reconsideration of the theological position of the Church. At this time there was the beginning of a trend which claimed that the Anglican Church in England was not the English nation in its spiritual aspect but that she was the representative in England of the Church Catholic and Apostolic, having as the chief cornerstone Jesus Christ and basing her doctrine and practice on His authority. In the Assize Sermon, John Keble said, "How can they possibly continue their communion with the Church Established (hither to the pride and comfort of their lives) without acquiring any of the taint of those Erastian principles on which she is now avowedly to be governed". He regarded the Church and the State as being quite separate--even as opposing forces. In an age when Catholic emancipation and other broadening principles were being discussed and acted upon there was a need to rethink the concept of Church and State. There was for Keble and his fellows a certain ambiguity in the concept of the governing of the Church. Why should Jews, Roman Catholics and Methodists be deciding what the Anglican Church should be doing in the realm of liturgy or in any other area of Church life? These were the burning questions of the day. Keble merely wanted to see the Church come alive and acquire again the spirit of fervency that she once had. The sermon on "National Apostasy" in 1833 certainly did start men thinking. Groups began to meet to discuss the pros and cons of this concept of the Apostolic Church. John Keble probably did not realize at the beginning just how quickly this movement would spread.

BACKGROUND

There are many reasons why at this particular point in history men should begin to be deeply concerned with the position of the Church. The stress that had been based on reason in the Eighteenth Century was becoming rather tiresome now and in a way faith in reason was beginning to collapse. There were new attitudes toward science, which were in many ways out of tune with the thinking of the past century. This was an age when there was a growing sympathy with the Dark Ages or at least with Medieval thought as is evidenced in the work of Byron, Shelley, Keats and a myriad others. There seemed to be an inherent desire to submit to authority. At any rate the intellectual climate seemed to be just right for a revival of some aspects of medieval thought. This Romantic spirit was evident not only in England, but all over Europe, and the Oxford Movement really must be understood in the light of this greater trend.

The Romantic revival affected literature, art, and philosophy as well as faith. It was a looking backward from the cold calculating attitudes of the eighteenth century to the depth and understanding of previous centuries. Men were becoming less interested in finding evidence to support everything and they were reaching out for faith. It was not as difficult as one would at first imagine trying to kindle interest in medieval doctrine because 'contemporary doctrine was held in such slight esteem. For many, there was a relaxed interest in the Protestant Reformers and a turning toward the Roman Church since she was so much more intimately bound up with the spirit of medieval thought. A large number of poets and artists went over to the Roman Church at this time in an attempt to recapture the medieval ethos. The leaders of the Oxford

Movement were most influenced by the French reactionaries. In France the priest had a rather prominent role in government; sacrilege was punished and the monasteries were restored. These things were somewhat appealing to the Oxford Fathers. There was a much more sceptical eye cast on the German scene. Along with this awakening interest in the medieval we find quite naturally a growing interest in the supernatural and the miraculous.

PROTESTANT ATTITUDES

Throughout all the history of the Anglican Communion perhaps one could say that in the time of the Oxford Fathers the leaning toward Protestantism was at its highest. Many factors tended to impair the strength of the Establishment and among them were the Wesleyan revivals, the Industrial Revolution, and the influence of Deism. It must be made absolutely clear at this point, however, that the writer is not deriding the work of John Wesley—the work that he did and the work that was done by the Oxford Reformers was directed toward the same end—the instilling of new life and fervour in the Church. The Oxford Reformers felt the need to concentrate partly upon the intellectual void that was present in the Church since the time of Wesley, for even though Wesley had done wonders to bring the common man into a very personal relationship with the Creator, he "was as remote as a man could be from the intellectual life of his time". (Quote: H. Stewart in A Century of Anglo-Catholicism.) For Wesley, to a large extent, man's learning was a menace to his faith. Wesley himself would not even study mathematics because he believed it would damage his religious beliefs. After Wesley's death the only group within the Anglican Church that still had any life was a group, which was almost indistinguishable from the Wesleyans. A great deal of Wesleyan teaching in regard to the life of holiness and morality was based on rather silly stories of people who had disobeyed the commands of God and who had subsequently been dealt with by God himself. An example of this is the story of a man who, on his way home from a dance, was struck by lightening. The coldness of the Established Church was enough to deter this sort of thinking but the result was not much better. The Church seemed often to be very cold and lifeless. Bishops and priests had been invested with quasi-imperial power making the Church seem almost feudal in nature.

With the gathering of skilled labourers in the cities and the rise of the middle classes, more and more of the leaders were from Nonconformist backgrounds thus making the Church of England a very weak social force. Deism was not the answer either. It had spent its strength before the nineteenth century had begun. By the time the Oxford Movement was starting to roll, Deism was teaching a doctrine that was very dry and tasteless. They had pushed intellectualism to the most absurd extremes. Newman remarked on one occasion that "the talent of the age is against the Church". In Germany the theological picture was also one of extremism where heresy seemed to be the ideal. The Oxford Fathers above all wanted to communicate faith.

CHIEF FIGURES OF THE MOVEMENT

John Keble, who is connected so closely to the Oxford Movement, because in a sense he sparked it, was the son of a country vicar. He was educated in the home of his father, who had, been a scholar and fellow of Corpus Christi College, along with his younger brother Tom. The Keble family was very closely knit and John grew up with a deep sense of respect for his parents. At the age of 14 he went to Corpus Christi on a scholarship and there he made many warm and lasting friendships. He was a most amiable person with very set opinions and he endeavoured at all costs to avoid controversy, however, when he could not possibly side step the issue he was very likely to lose his temper. On one occasion he went visiting with a friend to the home of a family who had become involved in what John called "heresy". He refused even to enter the house and he waited for his friend sitting on the front porch.

Keble seemed not to be able to distinguish between a man's character and his opinions. To him badness was stupidity. Even though he was quite shy and awkward he had a faculty for making almost every word he spoke seem tremendously significant.

One of the achievements for which John Keble is noted is his religious poetry. He wrote a book of such work, which was published under the title "The Christian Year" which was by many considered to be very fine poetry. Others felt that it lacked somewhat in technical skill and that if it had not been religious poetry it would have sunk quickly into oblivion. One critic even had the effrontery to remark that Keble's poetry sounded like Wordsworth translated for women.

In 1815 John was ordained and he went to be his father's curate where he lived quietly for a short time. It was not long before he was offered a tutorship at Oriel where the excitement was to take place. It is here where Keble and Hurrell Froude were to meet as teacher and pupil. Newman was also soon to enter the picture and with this curious mixture the ferment was inevitable.

PUSEY

Edward Bouverie Pusey grew up in a very religious atmosphere and as far back as he could remember he had entertained the idea that he would someday be a clergyman. His family background was one of serious scholarship and intense churchmanship. At Oxford he poured himself into his studies and did exceptionally well. John Keble was one of Pusey's examiners and it was here that they developed an intimate friendship. After a trip to the Continent, Edward went up to Oriel and here he came into contact with Newman. On another trip to Germany where he went to learn the language of that country, Pusey came into contact with the theological trends of the day. Here he was introduced to textual criticism, which in some ways frightened him. He read the works of Schleiermacher, was pleased with his work in some ways, but rather shocked in others. Pusey knew full well that these new ideas would eventually get to England.

NEWMAN

John Henry Newman was born on February 21, 1801 into a family that quite possibly had a Jewish background. The shape of his nose was probably the chief reason for even suspecting such a thing. Some of Newman's friends came to his defence in this matter and suggested that perhaps his background was not Jewish after all but Roman. Newman's father was a very religious man who was quite liberal in his views. There were times when quarrels of a minor nature broke out over religious questions. These were of course more frequent when the bank, with which Newman's father worked, was failing. John's mother was a devout woman of very strong will who's discipline undoubtedly helped to mould John's character. As John grew older he became increasingly more self assured, more philosophical and more superior. At the age of 15 he recalls having a conversion experience at which time he firmly believed that he had been "elected" by God. This idea gradually faded away and was for all intents and purposes gone by the time he became twenty-one. However, he knew that something had happened between God and his soul even if it wasn't a real conversion in the Evangelical sense. It seemed to be rather a fusion of intellect and feeling. It was at this time that John Henry Newman made a decision regarding celibacy.

After obtaining a Fellowship at Oriel, Newman went and served a curacy in the slums of Oxford. He returned finally to the university as a tutor and became the rector of St. Mary's, the university Church, where he won a reputation as a preacher of note. It was here where Newman came in contact with the High Churchmen and where he began to become intensely interested in the authority of the Church and in Apostolic Succession. He came to regard the Church as a Divine Society, which was really quite apart from the State.

The concept that tradition was necessary for Christian belief and that the Bible does not so much teach doctrine but rather proves doctrine gained a firm foothold in his thinking. After much opposition and unhappiness Newman began to doubt the validity of the Anglican position and he finally resigned his parish. Two years later he went to the Roman Church. He had spent forty-five years in the Anglican Church, and he had yet another forty-five years within the fold of the Roman Church. Some people speculate that Newman declined as an orator after he went to the Roman Church, some even claiming that Newman himself realized this. Actually he once admitted himself that his 'Protestant' works had seen much more success than his Catholic ones.

FROUDE

Hurrell Froude also played quite a significant role in the first years of the Movement. His life was one of exuberant energy. Some feel that he burned himself out with all his sailing and riding. When he gradually became worse and worse in health, he was advised to go abroad to a warmer, dryer climate to attempt to regain his health. He spent some time in the Mediterranean and on the island of Barbados in the West Indies. One of the most notable things that Froude did for the Movement was to help Newman and Keble understand one another better. Keble had distrusted Newman in the beginning. The chief source of information concerning Froude's life is his work "<u>Remains</u>".

THE TRACTS

The Oxford Movement was an attempt to reconcile the static and the dynamic in many ways. The leaders of the Movement sought unceasingly to win back for the Church a sense of holiness that seemed to have disappeared from the scene. The dualism that was causing the tension was that between the State and the Church— the life of the Empire and that of the spirit. This is what Newman was determined to sort out. Newman was very much of the belief that "fore-ordination" or God's "foreknowledge" had something quite important to do with the whole situation. He believed that the Gospel had come, not simply to make people better citizens or more agreeable people, but that it had come to perfect the natural in us and to make us members of the New Jerusalem. This is undoubtedly why Newman, as well as the other Fathers of the Movement, was concerned with the doctrine of the Communion of Saints and in the life beyond the grave—the Resurrection.

Dr. Pusey outlined the trends and hopes of the Movement in a very concise way:

i.) a high regard for the sacraments

ii.) a high regard for the episcopacy

iii.) a high regard for the visible Church

iv.) a visible devotion (Physical and practical)

v.) a reverence for the Ancient Church.

The Tracts (after which the Movement was sometimes called the "Tractarian Movement") were short treatises on various subjects often written in a very stark manner. Newman was the first to begin publishing these tracts, which he called "Tracts for the Times". He wrote 23 of these himself and soon the other enthusiasts of the group began to contribute also. The tracts encouraged doctrines that were unquestionably ancient but which were popularly associated with the Church of Rome and it was partly this that led to so many of their problems. Some of the ideas that were pressed were the regenerative nature of the sacrament of baptism, the importance of tradition in Christian thinking and the sacrificial nature of the Eucharist. Tract XC was concerned with the Thirty-nine Articles of Religion and it was this one that finally caused a considerable reaction. It proved to be the last of the Tracts.

As has already been mentioned, the style of the tracts was very stark, much the same as was Newman's preaching. Even though Newman was a rather monotonous speaker he was able to hold the congregation of St. Mary's Church spellbound. This was probably because he possessed a certain ability to see into the human mind and because he was a master of the English language. Many feel that he purposely spoke as he did in Church in an attempt to remove his personality and allow the Church to speak. In support of their doctrines and teachings, the Tractarians "ransacked the works of

Hooker, Jewell, of Andrewes, of Ken, and of Jeremy Taylor." (H, A. Stewart, <u>A Century of Anglo-Catholicism.</u>) They regarded these men as part of the valuable tradition of the English Church. Thinking of this sort had so long been neglected that it was, for the Anglican Church of the mid-eighteen hundreds, a veritable novelty. Restoration rather than innovation was the aim of the Oxford Reformers. Occasionally the tracts went quite overboard to prove a point and it was then that they became ridiculous. To the mind of these men it was the ultra-protestants who were departing from the spirit of Anglicanism, not they themselves.

TRACT XC

Tract XC was an attempt to show that the 39 Articles of Religion could be interpreted in a very catholic manner—in fact it states that the Articles could be shown to be completely in harmony with the Tridentine decrees. Newman claimed that the Articles are quite indefinite in their expression and that very vague language is used. His belief that the Church must have a standard by which to measure her doctrine is expressed here. That the Articles are this standard and that they do express the Catholic faith is also stated here. This whole pattern of thought naturally raised the question of just what the word catholic meant. Did it mean Roman Catholic? It undoubtedly meant, 'the official Roman position as set forth at the Council of Trent'. The Articles certainly reject the third of these concepts—the "Romish doctrines", but what of the other two? There were many and diverse opinions about this.

Storm clouds gathered over England with the publication of Tract XC and Bishop Bagot of Oxford, under pressure from Canterbury, took action to have the tracts stopped. In a letter to the Bishop, Newman claimed complete loyalty to the Anglican Church. In defence of this movement there was a deluge of writing sparked by the action taken against Tract XC. It has been suggested that Newman was, in Tract XC, trying to convince himself as much as anyone else that the position of the Anglican Church was compatible with Catholic thought. The Anglican Church, he believed, was much more allied to Rome than to Protestantism. It cannot be denied that the Articles have a decided leaning toward the Protestant point of view as they were written in a time when the Church was trying to combat certain ideas that were considered to be extreme; for instance the Lutheran idea that man is justified when he believes himself to be justified (Article XI), and in Article XX, on the Authority of the Church, ("The Church hath power to decree Rites or Ceremonies, and Authority in controversies of Faith...."). This certainly underscores the Puritan preference for minimizing in matters of ceremonial against the Papist exaggeration in matters of doctrine.

There was a certain amount of strain put on the more Protestant minded clergy by the language of the Prayer Book and on the other hand a strain on the Tractarians by the tenor and wording of the Thirty-Nine Articles. An example of the Catholic teaching and practice that is enshrined in the Book of Common Prayer is the provision for full auricular confession in the order of the Ministry to the Sick. Another example is the very prayer of ordination itself:

> "Receive the Holy Ghost for the office and work of a Priest in the Church of God now

committed unto thee by the imposition of our hands. Whose sins thou dost forgive, they are forgiven; and whose sins thou dost retain, they are retained. And be thou a faithful dispenser of the Word of God, and of his holy Sacraments. In the Name of the Father, and of the Son, and of the Holy Ghost. Amen."

The Tractarians were able to point these things out and demand of the non-Tractarians an explanation of their significance. The Tracts were not really concerned with the actual matters of ritual —that is regarding the use of incense, acolytes and vestments, but these concerns did become part of the ethos of the movement. A modern reader going strictly from the evidence that is presented in the Tracts would in all likelihood not consider the Movement to have been very radical at all. This, of course, is partly due to the fact that so many of the issues for which the Movement stood have become part and parcel of Anglicanism, as it exists today.

To the public mind of the day one of the greatest irritants was the apparent hostility toward the Reformation. This came to the surface most noticeably when Keble and Newman published the <u>Remains,</u> a work by Hurrell Froude. He had made the remark "odious Protestantism sticks in people's gizzard", and other equally pointed comments. Another problem that seemed to be somewhat contradictory was that, even as the Tractarians were championing the authority of the Church and the adherence to the liturgy, they were in opposition to the Thirty-Nine Articles which themselves were the "authority of the Church". That the Articles could be interpreted in the light of the ancient Church was, of course, what the Movement was claiming at every opportunity.

CEREMONIAL

That aspect of the Oxford Movement concerning ceremonial, which is often mistaken for the whole of the movement, began very quietly to creep in around 1857-8. It was not something peculiar to Oxford. This other movement which was interested in restoring Church architecture and furnishings had begun in Cambridge and was actually a much wider movement than was Oxford at that time. Those who were involved in this movement were interested in turning churches into houses of prayer rather than meeting halls. They turned to the medieval centuries for guidance in this respect.

> "It was another part of that almost universal turning from the head towards the heart. Its roots lay in the desire to turn the churches into houses of prayer and devotion, where men would let their hearts go outward and upward in worship, instead of preaching-houses where their minds would he argued into an assent to creeds or moral duties."

This whole way of thinking encouraged the idea of more frequent communions and the recitation of the daily offices. Altar hangings befitting the ecclesiastical seasons (penitential for Lent and rich for festivals) and coloured stoles were encouraged. These things today are thought to be irrelevant or wrong only by a minimal number of Anglicans. It must be stressed again, however, that the key figures in the Movement (Keble, Pusey and Newman) were themselves really not very concerned with these things.

INFLUENCE OF THE MOVEMENT

The Oxford Movement has changed the face of the Anglican Communion both externally and internally. It has affected both the religious, devotional and theological life of Anglicans throughout the world. The content of prayer has become much more enriched as people become increasingly aware of the treasures of Catholic centuries. However, in honesty it can be said the Movement has failed to change the religious beliefs of Englishmen.

The success of the movement has been very marked in the realm of liturgical reform. Much was gained by design but untold advances were made incidentally. The movement seems to have been all that was necessary to disturb the ecclesiastical lethargy and spark interest in the whole realm of church life. As well as the liturgical reform mentioned above, church music and architecture began to have some very necessary attention paid to them.

Actually it would probably be more truthful to say that, at least in the area of liturgics, there was not so much improvement or innovation as there was a return to earlier practises. This is of course because of the fact that since approximately the time of the Second English Prayer Book there had been such bad liturgical scholarship. Men were now freeing themselves from the old Puritan view that aids to the eye or the other senses were automatically considered to be evil. It was at this time that men realized that they could effectively worship the Creator with the whole self. Another blessing that came of the Oxford Movement was the present decent appearance of clerical attire. This has affected clergy of almost all denominations. Members of the Roman Catholic Church have also benefited insofar as they have been more sympathetically understood by many Protestants. This is, in a sense, because Anglo-Catholics appreciate the importance of the liturgical and sacramental life and yet are not Roman.

The episcopate was, at the beginning of the Movement, a subject of argument and was by many considered a novel idea. Many clergy (including Bishops) did not really consider the episcopate an important feature of the Church. The second tract was a particularly foolish tirade about the problem of the ten Irish bishoprics. The government obviously had full right to reduce the number of sees in that part of the country. Many of these sees had been placed there as coast guard stations and police-barracks were set up—besides, the Church in these areas had been particularly dead.

One of the admirable qualities that the Anglo-Catholic movement has instilled in the life of the English Church is the spirit of independence and spiritual freedom. It has allowed Churchmen to get away from the sort of ethos where the keynote is a sentimental kind of morality and has encouraged them to move into one where decisiveness dominates.

Tract I certainly typified this spirit when it shrieked out in bold capitals "HE THAT IS NOT WITH ME IS AGAINST ME, and he that gathereth not with me scattereth abroad." There has of course been a certain amount of criticism aimed at the Oxford Apostles for being somewhat obstinate in their views, but perhaps it is far more important to hold definite views than to simply muddle through not saying anything in either direction. One of the detrimental developments of the Movement has been the tendency of some to drift toward pure ritualism—the sort with no backbone of solid theology. This is the sort of thing that often offends and appals Free Churchmen. It has in some instances been a detriment in discussions of union and has generally hampered relations between Anglicans and non-Anglicans.

One development that may be a credit to the Anglo-Catholic position is that almost all of the work done amongst the poorer areas in the larger English cities in the past century has been done by either the very evangelical Christians or by Anglo-Catholics. In other words the Anglo-Catholic party has proven to be very evangelical in its outlook—which perhaps sounds rather confusing to the minds of some because unfortunately, and quite wrongly, the word "evangelical" has come to be attached to another particular brand of churchmanship.

Perhaps the most important thing that the Oxford Movement has taught the Church is that a worshipping community can only understand itself in the light of its own history and continuity.

REFLECTIONS ON THE OXFORD MOVEMENT
JUNE 2012

Whatever had caused me to become interested in the church led me to begin shopping around in our district which I mentioned in the Reflections on the chapter dealing with the Eucharist. Initially, I assumed that all Anglican Churches must be similar to St. Andrew's until that evening when I was invited to attend a friend's confirmation service, also previously mentioned.

This was my first exposure to the Anglo-Catholic aspect of the Anglican Church and it has truly had a lifelong and fundamental influence on what constitutes my very nature. I was from that point on caught up in everything that poured forth from the experience and it has shaped so much of my life.

My paternal grandparents immigrated to Canada in 1910 from England and came to settle in Sapperton, then a small village near New

Westminster which was the hub of life in British Columbia in those days. They were Church of England and soon found a happy community of likeminded English folk in the parish church of St. Mary the Virgin in that small town. Probably, at that time, a goodly number of the Caucasian residents of British Columbia were of British extraction.

Even before I came to know anything about the Anglican Church I had heard my grandmother discussing how the Vicar of St. Mary's, Mr. Plaskett, had introduced the surplice. I assume that the clergy and choir wore the black academic or Geneva gown in those days not so long after the influences of the Tractarian Movement. After becoming acquainted with St. James' I began to realize that the Diocese of New Westminster, in its early days, had quite a catholic foundation and numbers of catholic minded clergy and bishops. In fact, I believe that the diocese had been founded by such adventuresome people in the 1850s and 60s.

In the far eastern part of the diocese at Yale, near the lower end of the Fraser Canyon, a group of Sisters from England had come to found a school for young ladies, which would compliment the Industrial School for boys at Lytton which was a little further up the Fraser Canyon road. The Sisters were from the Community of All Hallows in Ditchingham, Norfolk and came at the request of Bishop Acton Sillitoe, first Bishop of the Diocese of New Westminster.

St. James' parish in Vancouver was the first church to be established in the tiny town of Hastings Mill on Burrard Inlet. The town would change names a number of times—Hastings Mill, Gastown, Granville, and finally Vancouver. The Great Fire of 1886 levelled the town in a single day including the tiny St. James' mission on the waterfront. Everything was rather quickly rebuilt and the Canadian Pacific Railway provided land not far from St. James' original location for a much larger wood-frame building. Eventually, that would be replaced in 1936 by the present reinforced concrete building, which is one of the gems of Vancouver architecture.

It was to this church I was invited to witness my friend's confirmation and it was to be the beginning of a long association culminating in my eventually being an assistant priest there for the last ten years of my ministry.

On the evening of that confirmation service in the 1950s I had no idea what to expect. I suppose I simply assumed it would be rather like my own parish in Burnaby. I had been given a ride to the church, which is in the skid-road part of Vancouver, and after parking the car we made our way up the front steps into the beauty of holiness, which was this special place. The pungent odour of beeswax, incense and the kerosene oil of the sanctuary lamps filled my mind with beautiful associations. The pipe organ quietly played some dreamy, impressionistic, French liturgical music before the service and the atmosphere was quiet and prayerful. Finally, the congregation stood as the Bishop's Procession entered from the north aisle. The Bishop was vested in a beautiful green cope and mitre led by acolytes with incense and torches. With an organ fanfare the Bishop was escorted to his seat in the sanctuary. Soon the clergy, more servers and the candidates entered the church in another procession and the liturgy began. It was the same bishop who had confirmed me some six months before, but one would hardly have guessed that this was the same church. I was held spellbound and captivated.

As an aside, I should add here a fact that probably bears heavily on my reaction to this experience. During the past two years I have accidentally discovered that I have, in all likelihood, Asperger's Syndrome. I realized this while looking at entries about it on YouTube while surfing randomly. A young Swedish man was explaining what it is like to have Asperger's. (The English have a way of pronouncing this word with a soft 'g' and putting the stress on the penultimate syllable so that it doesn't sound quite like "Assburgers"). It is classed as an autism spectrum disorder but I think that it is really more akin to a personality type. I eventually found on the internet an evaluation to confirm whether one has this 'disorder' or not, and I scored quite positively for having it. It explains a lot about my personality and quirks and I find it quite helpful to know this. It also gives me leave to blame so many things on 'my Aspbergers'.

One of the many symptoms is a heightened attraction to order. I attribute my tastes and preferences in liturgy to this. The person with Aspberger's also feels extra sensitive to outside stimulus as in too much light or sound. For instance I find it extremely difficult to converse with people in a large crowd where there is loud chattering. I find I can't really hear them over the din of the many other conversations, all of which sound loud and blurring to me. It seems to create an extraordinarily stressful and distracting ambiance. "Too much input", said the young man in the video.

Some of the other markers of Aspberger's Syndrome are: lack of empathy, uncoordinated motor movements, rigid thinking and fear of changes, overly formal speech patterns and sometimes inappropriate and unsolicited candid remarks. Many of these attributes I recognize in myself, although not every person exhibits all of these symptoms. However, I do see that many of these things have had a hand in my making certain choices with regard to being involved in the Church and specifically with the Anglo-Catholic part of it.

In the first years of my journey in the church I recall that in the diocese there were only four parishes where eucharistic vestments were used—and the chasuble was certainly the undisputed sign of a theology of the sacrificial aspect of the eucharist. How liturgical fashions have changed! Now it is quite common that clergy of any church whatever use full eucharistic vestments in their worship—and sometimes even when the worship is not eucharistic. They seem not to have the slightest idea what the vestments represent, other than that they are pretty. Most certainly this foray into liturgy is not at all what John Henry Newman would have recognized as *catholic* in any sense of the word.

Generally today Anglican congregations seem to have tried to become less formal and more community minded in worship. The day seems to have passed when before Mass there would be a lot of silence, meditating and preparation. Even during the actual celebration there seems to be less care taken for promoting an atmosphere of spirituality.

It is difficult to believe that at St. James' in the early 1950s the High Mass at 11:15 am was a non-communicating Mass except for a few who were elderly or disabled. It was in essence an offering of adoration and worship. These were the days of less frequent reception, however, anyone wishing to receive communion would also have attended an earlier Mass as well as having probably made confession. It is quite amazing how much Vatican II had an impact upon the Anglican Communion. It also causes me to shudder a little that I have seen such change in my lifetime and it causes me to feel considerably more aware of my age.

Rereading this essay again I thoroughly regret one thing in particular. It was intended to examine the theological aspects of the Oxford Movement and to consider what new visions it brought to the established English Church. It naturally in addition raised quite a furore from some quarters within the Establishment. But, the aspect, which is rather missing from my college treatment of the subject, is the depth of the social implications that accompanied the liturgical and theological concerns. Granted, the essay does end with a sketchy paragraph, which makes reference to the social dynamics, but that aspect of the Movement is without a doubt vital and integral to the whole thrust of that which began in Oxford.

Another essay could easily have been devoted to the invaluable work and slogging that those valiant priests did for the people they served in the ghettos and slums of London Docks, Manchester, Birmingham and the depressed parts of so many English cities, especially those areas involved in industrial and mining pursuits.

The theological and philosophical elements of the Oxford Movement were more than adequately dealt with by the scholastics, Newman, Pusey, Froude and Keble, but there were also hundreds of other heroic priests who gave their lives so devotedly and completely to the work in their parishes and to the people living in those places. It frequently meant becoming involved in labour disputes, educational problems as well as medical and housing issues—in fact, literally in every aspect of the lives of their people.

I will mention here, in a somewhat abbreviated form, just two of those heroes—Fathers Charles Lowder and Alexander Mackonochie whose lives and work became frequently intertwined. In 1858 Father Mackonochie moved to become a curate at St George's-in-the-East, London. There it was that he first worked with Charles Lowder as a mission priest in the slum area of the Thames Docks. At this time St. George's-in-the-East was a focus for anti-Ritualist rioting which involved services being interrupted and stones being thrown at the mission's priests.

In 1862 Father Mackonochie became curate at St. Alban the Martyr, Holborn. He introduced daily communion, which featured Gregorian chant and other ritual elements such as the lighting of

Altar candles and the cleansing of Eucharistic vessels at the Altar. St. Alban's was the first Anglican Church ever to hold the three-hour devotion of the Passion on Good Friday. Mackonochie also made it known that he would be happy to hear confessions. His pastoral ministry was typical of the 19th-century ritualist "slum priest". With his two curates, Arthur Stanton and Edward Russell, and lay assistants he founded schools, soup kitchens, a working men's club, mother's meetings, clothing funds and more. Throughout his later persecution, St. Alban's remained a thriving Anglo-Catholic parish. From 1867 Mackonochie was also chaplain of the Sisterhood of St. Saviour and the sisters of the Clewer Community of St. John Baptist, who worked in the parish. St. Alban's increasingly became a focus of Low Church ire.

In 1882 a new round of prosecutions was under way when, on the deathbed request of Archbishop Tait, Mackonochie resigned from St. Alban's to move to St. Peter's, London Docks, the church founded 1866 by C.F. Lowder. By 1882 the mob violence that Mackonochie had faced during his time with Lowder in the 1850s and 1860s had abated but the prosecutions continued.

Father Charles Lowder was ordained a deacon on Michaelmas 1843 and became a curate at Walton near Glastonbury. He was ordained a priest in 1844 by Bishop Denison of Salisbury and became chaplain of the Axbridge workhouse. From 1845 to 1851 he was curate of Tetbury, Gloucestershire. However, Lowder wished to move to a parish with a more Catholic pattern of worship and in 1851 he became assistant curate to James Skinner at St. Barnabas' Church, Pimlico. St. Barnabas', a chapel of ease to St. Paul's Knightsbridge was at the time at the vanguard of the Ritualist movement. The church lay at the heart of an area of slums, having been built to serve the poor.

Fr. Lowder seems to have had endless skirmishes with anti-ritualist enthusiasts and with the law courts on numbers of occasions and often being suspended from service. It seems that there has always been some sort of friction or other concerning theological issues in Anglican circles, including those that continue to this day regarding dissent about doctrine or, what is more probably the case, the quest for dominance and authority.

This style of Christian worship and ministry resonates with me to the very core of my being.

Large portions of my own vocation as a priest have been realized in connection with disadvantaged people and this has enabled me to experience both the agony and the ecstasy of living, strengthened by the spirituality of the faith. I have alluded to some of these situations in previous chapters.

✠

The final ten years of my working life were spent in a rather idyllic setting—the parish which as a teenager I discovered, and which had such a profound impact upon my thinking and aspirations. It was situated right in the middle of Canada's most allegedly depressed neighbourhood —Skid Road! So many times I have heard this section of Vancouver described as Canada's most depressed postal code designation. The area has been that way, I understand, from almost the very beginnings of the City of Vancouver. The Parish has, from its inception in the days of Father Henry Fiennes Clinton, been a bastion of Anglo-Catholic devotion and teaching. He was perhaps one of the first or second-generation Oxford Movement priests. The Parish became, by my time there, an influential element in the Diocese of New

Westminster offering excellence in liturgy, music and spirituality in addition to championing the way into avenues, which were central to the needs of local residents.

In the late 50s or early 60s, a parishioner asked the then Rector, Father David Somerville, if the parish could provide a room in the church hall basement so that she could work with local residents—mostly at that time, men on welfare or small pensions—an alternative to their typically squalid rooms in local hotels. The room where they would meet eventually became known as the "Pensioners' Room". The lady was May Gutteridge, and so it began, one woman with a vision and a small gathering of rag-tag neighbours. May, often referred to as Mrs. G, would assist these men with matters such as budgeting their funds, paying rent, buying food and a host of other life-issues.

To make a long story a little shorter, over the course of the next forty years this work grew and grew, as May often said, "like Topsy". It eventually developed into the St. James' Social Service Society, which is still the leading light of social work and development in Vancouver's East End.

During my years at St. James', the three staff clergy lived in the Clergy House adjoining the church and each of us had special involvement with various groups and organizations as Chaplains and advisors. It was my privilege, and sometimes anguish, to have spent seven years as Chaplain and board member of St. James' Social Service. At that time the Society had holdings in shops and hotels along Powell Street as well as facilities in other parts of the city and employed at one time over two hundred staff members. Needless to say, the Society was assisted and subsidized by the Provincial Government. The anguish part of my experience came as we dealt with moving into the computer age; adopting current accounting procedures and with problems and tricky manoeuvres related to unions and employment structures.

Mrs. Gutteridge retired during my time on the Board, but I can still hear her saying as she often did about the Society, that "everything we do here at St. James' (Social Service) flows from the altar". May was, of course, a fixture at the High Mass every Sunday, and since she died some years ago has been given a feast day in St. James' Parish calendar.

With reference to the kind of relationship and influence the parish had with the ongoing life all around it, I should explain that the Angelus was rung each day on the tenor bell in our tower, just before Mass at seven in the morning, at noon and after Evensong at six in the evening, thus reminding the neighbourhood that the Incarnation is a reality in the everyday routine of the community. The Remand Centre and Law Courts were just across the street from St. James.

One evening, preceding the monthly Trustees' meeting we were sitting with several of the members, including Justice Herbert Oliver, having a cocktail before we gathered in the Church Hall for our meeting. Judge Oliver, who was an extremely amusing and eloquent man, who always reminded me of Lawrence Olivier or some such Thespian, was holding 'court' and regaling us with his clever wit.

On this occasion he told us about a time when he was presiding over a case in one of the courtrooms across the street in the late morning. It was a fairly minor case involving a miscreant who had been charged with shoplifting or some such infraction. The time came for the sentencing and just at that moment the noon Angelus rang out from St. James' tower. He recounted how humbled he was and what the announcement of the Incarnation meant to him and he decided at the last moment to reduce the sentence somewhat, considering that the Prince of Peace had taken flesh for this man too.

EIGHT

THE MISSIONARY WORK OF WILLIAM DUNCAN OF METLAKATLA AND JAMES McCULLAGH OF AIYANSH

Church History III
November 9, 1967

Anglican Missionary activity in the Pacific Northwest could be said to have started when the Church Missionary Society sent out a young lay worker by the name of William Duncan in the mid-eighteen hundreds. This story is one of fantastic perseverance and hardship as well as one of personal striving and ultimate failure.

William Duncan decided to devote his life to the mission of the Church in Canada as the result of an appeal made during a meeting of the Church Missionary Society on a stormy, wet evening. He was a schoolmaster at the time and he had prepared for this profession at the Highbury Training College. He was offered passage to his field of work by Captain Prevost of the man-of-war "H.M.S. Satellite". Captain Prevost had previously been to the Pacific Northwest, had seen the people native to the area and was very concerned about their "deplorable and heathen" existence. The trip around the Horn took some six months and upon arriving in Esquimault, on the southern tip of Vancouver Island, Duncan found that he would have to wait there for three months until passage could be secured for Fort Simpson. Finally it was found and he arrived in Fort Simpson amongst the Tsimshean Indians faced with seemingly impossible work ahead of him. Many people had tried to persuade Duncan that he should abandon the plan altogether. The officials of the Hudson's Bay Company and others felt that he was doing a very unwise thing. He found a supporter, however in Captain Prevost and he managed to continue on. In Fort Simpson Duncan found a Company stockade with a staff of 20 white men and breeds. The Tsimshean Indians lived outside the fort and were never allowed in.

To leave the fort was considered sudden death. The Tsimshean Indians were quite warlike and were also cannibalistic.

Duncan began his work by conducting Sunday services and running a school, which was at first just for the residents of the fort. Soon he was to allow Indian children to enter for study then eventually the adult Indians. Soon after beginning his work he ventured outside the palisade to conduct a survey of the Native population. He managed to visit every single home and discovered that there were some 250 wooden houses and well over 2000 Indians. Duncan was to witness the murder and eating of a slave woman, which of course horrified him and spurred him on to convert these people from their heathen ways to the Christian Faith. Much of his time during the first months of his stay was occupied in learning the language of the people. A young Indian by the name of Clah helped him in this endeavour and after eight months Duncan was ready to attempt a sermon in Tsimshean. He went to each of the chief's houses and spoke to groups of about 100 to 150 and he found that they were most respectful and attentive.

He was surprised to find that the Indians knelt at his request spontaneously. To Duncan this indicated that they had some idea of prayer and of what he was speaking about. Just before delivering his first sermon he had a sudden fear that he would not be able to manage it and he asked Clah to deliver the sermon instead. The shock that registered on Clah's face soon put an end to that idea. One of the chiefs was a particularly wicked man according to Duncan, however, he commanded his people to be silent and to listen to the preacher. The medicine men of the tribe were particularly unhappy with the influence that Duncan was having on their people and his life was in constant danger because of this. After a year and a half there was a very noticeable change in the people to whom Duncan was ministering. Even Legaic, the chief who had been such an opponent, appeared at the school anxious to learn.

Three years after Duncan had arrived in Fort Simpson the Church Missionary Society sent the Rev L. S. Tugwell to work in the same area. He baptized the first converts on July 26, 1861. Bishop Hills was the first bishop to come to British Columbia. He took up residence in Victoria and was responsible for the whole of the province. The later controversy involving Dean Cridge of Victoria was not very helpful in dealing with Duncan who seems to have grown more and more unhappy with the authority structure of the Church. It seems that Cridge and Duncan were close friends.

Work in Fort Simpson seemed to be constantly held back because of the nearness of the heathen Indians. Duncan gradually conceived of the idea of leaving for a place away from other people where he could establish his religious colony. He felt that his sheep would be much safer away from the "miasma" of heathen life. The Natives were to be kept from visiting Victoria except on lawful business. This is the point at which one would almost immediately think that Duncan was trying to form a Victorian moral community rather than a Christian community, but perhaps at that particular time the distinction was difficult to make. The location for the new community was pointed out by the Indians themselves. It was a place from which many of them had come years before they went to live in Simpson. It was situated some 17 miles from Fort Simpson on an inland channel which was protected from the weather and also, which was probably most important in the mind of Duncan, away from the trading ships. The name of this village was to be

Metlakatla, the name by which it had previously been known.

On May 27, 1862 Duncan and his party left for their new homestead. Only 50 people went with him initially, probably because of his very rigid rules, but they were soon joined by some 300 more who evidently reconsidered and decided to take the chance. The following are the rules that Duncan set up for his new community:

1) To give up their "Ahlied," or Indian deviltry

2) To cease calling in conjurers when sick

3) To cease gambling

4) To cease giving away their property for display

5) To cease painting their faces

6) To cease drinking intoxicating drink

7) To rest on the Sabbath

8) To attend religious instruction

9) To send their children to school

10) To be clean

11) To be industrious

12) To be peaceful

13) To be liberal and honest in trade

14) To build neat houses

15) To pay the village tax.

Metlakatla was to become a thriving centre with "Father Duncan" as the lay preacher. (It is strange that Duncan was referred to by the title "Father" because he seems to have resisted vigorously any hint of hierarchical structure and sacerdotalism. He is referred to by this name even to the present day by Natives of Metlakatla.) The Rev. Mr. Tugwell unfortunately returned to England after a relatively short stay, having contracted some sort of illness. Very few of the ordained men sent out by the CMS seem to have lasted for very long—which was probably quite a happy situation as far as William Duncan was concerned. Duncan fulfilled almost every possible capacity in his new colony. He was the treasurer of the settlement; clerk of the works, head schoolmaster, counsellor, preacher, magistrate and many other functions fell within his jurisdiction. There certainly seems to be no doubt that he worked ceaselessly and diligently for the people of Metlakatla.

In 1863 Bishop Hills made a journey to Metlakatla in order to baptize and celebrate the Eucharist. He made another visit three years later in 1866 and apart from these visits the village had no real episcopal ties. In the absence of an ordained man, Duncan himself baptized the cannibal chief Quthray who had been a particularly violent opponent of Duncan1s work. This man was curiously baptized Philip Atkinson. He was in fact one of the men who had eaten the slave woman when Duncan first came to Fort Simpson. Duncan reports how this man repented and wept over his sins. The fact that these people had at one time been cannibalistic proved to be quite a problem in the teaching of the faith in its fullness. Duncan, for instance, was hesitant to admit these people to the Holy Communion because he felt that they would make a fetish of it. Being taught that they were receiving the 'body and blood' of Jesus would in his mind lead to nothing but a mixture of the

Christian faith and the heathen notions of former years. This problem was of course brought out much more in the open when Bishop Ridley appears on the scene. Many people have tried to intimate that there was a churchmanship problem involved in this controversy but it certainly would seem that the real problem was one of teaching the faith of the Christian Church as it is expressed by the Church of England as opposed to the omission of certain basic principles of Christianity. Bishop Ridley and the other ordained men that were sent out by the CMS were hardly what one would call "High Church" even in those days shortly after the Oxford Movement had begun. CMS had always had a rather low church orientation.

In 1870 Duncan went to England to do work on his organization of the colony. He busied himself with learning rope making, brush making, twine spinning and many other arts that would be useful in his work at Metlakatla. He even learned how to play some 21 musical instruments.

All this time Duncan was alone with his people. As has already been pointed out, all of the men sent out from England soon gave in to the difficult living conditions or to poor health and returned home. Some of these were Tugwell, Doolan, Gribbell, and Tomlinson.

The controversy alluded to earlier, which involved Dean Cridge in Victoria, had quite a bad affect on Duncan. He was a friend of the Dean's and he was certainly no more endeared to the Church authorities when Cridge was, as Duncan believed, forced to leave the Church and join the Reformed Episcopal Church. This made it even more difficult to arrange for future episcopal visits to Metlakatla by any Bishop. Bishop Bompas made the long journey from Rupert's Land (near Hudson's Bay) over the Rockies to the Coast in order to minister to the episcopal needs of Metlakatla. While he was there he confirmed many and ordained William Collison who was appointed priest-in-charge of the mission. Of course as soon as the Bishop left there was no question of where the authority lay—it was still in the hands of Mr. Duncan, even though the CMS (Duncan's supposed authority) had confirmed the Bishops action.

Bishop Hills was in England in 1879 and he made arrangements for his diocese to be divided. It was divided into three parts forming two new dioceses. New Westminster and Caledonia. The Rev.

William Ridley (who had been a missionary in India) was elected and appointed first Bishop of Caledonia. After the long trip from England he arrived in Victoria to be met by Duncan and Admiral Prevost. They then journeyed onward together.

In the writings of Bishop Ridley we can see the magnitude of the complete authority that Duncan held in his colony. As far as Duncan was concerned the Bishop was merely an intruder. Unfortunately the Bishop could not do very much about it since he did not yet understand the Indian tongue. On Sundays he was merely another body in the congregation. Duncan reports how the Bishop robed even though he did not seem to have any authority. Naturally, Duncan saw the Bishop as a threat. It would seem to us now that Bishop Ridley was trying in the most diplomatic way to fulfil the role that he was supposed to have as the new Bishop of Caledonia. He must have been an exceedingly patient man. He writes that the town, as far as material progress is concerned, was making real headway but that the Church aspect was sadly neglected. There was no attempt to give the people the scriptures in their native tongue or to translate the Prayer Book into Tsimshean. Also there were no bible classes and all the addresses to the Indians were by Duncan or Collison. The stress on worldly possessions was increasing more and more all the time.

Reports managed to get out of Metlakatla indicating that there was a terrible "episcopal autocracy" attempting to overthrow the wonderful Christian work that Duncan was doing. Unfortunately it got into the hands of certain people who believed Duncan. The Bishop was very sharply criticized by the Methodists and the Presbyterians and even by many members of the Church of England. The Bishop often went far into the upper reaches of the Skeena Valley in order to avoid the terrible controversy that was growing. He simply had to stay away from Duncan.

Soon an ultimatum was issued by the Church Missionary Society ordering Duncan to; a) come to England for a conference, b) to begin a programme of teaching as Bishop Ridley had suggested, or c) hand over the mission to the Bishop. Duncan, however, did not answer the CMS. Instead he called the Indians together and announced that the CMS had released him. He asked the people where their loyalty was and it is not difficult to see why they unquestionably followed him. This particular incident is a little difficult to sort out after having read the accounts of it as it is described by John Arctander. Arctander was a supporter of Duncan who wrote the book The Apostle of Alaska. He claimed that the Bishop did not handle the situation very nicely and that he had tried to force Duncan to resign. Approximately 100 of the one thousand Indians remained faithful to the Bishop and they were very poorly treated. The Bishop immediately returned to England leaving his courageous wife behind. After the Bishop's return the two factions lived together for some five years without acknowledging each other. The Bishop and his followers were not allowed any place to conduct worship and they were completely snubbed on the streets. On one occasion, when Duncan was away in Victoria, the Bishop reports that Duncan's followers were very civil and kind to him, however as soon as Duncan returned it was the same old story.

Eventually Duncan and his people came into conflict with the government over land claims. There was a legal hassle and news of this got to the outside world. It was not too long before people began to realize that the unhappiness between the

Church and Duncan was not so much a conflict between "episcopal autocracy" and Christian liberty, but simply one between any authority and liberty.

Duncan made a trip to New York to appeal for sympathy and it was at this time that he came into contact with John Arctander. He even went so far as to visit the President to enlist his aid. In the name of his 500 Indians he renounced the Queen and promised never to fly the Union Jack again. He and his people were granted some land in American Territory (Annette Island) some 70 miles north of Metlakatla. Before leaving their old homestead they destroyed their houses and other public buildings.

The building of the huge church at New Metlakatla is one of the things about this story that seems incredible. The wooden building was extremely large (almost twice the size of the present Cathedral in Prince Rupert in what is now the Diocese of Caledonia) and could accommodate 700 worshippers. It was built entirely by the Indians with the guidance of Duncan. He himself marvelled at the fact that only a short time previously these same people had committed "fiendish acts". The first services were held in the new church (which was nick-named the Westminster Abbey of Metlakatla) on Christmas Day of 1874.

Soon after they left the Canadian Metlakatla, the remaining Indians asked the Bishop to explain to them the Biblical references to the Lord's Supper and it was not very long before they were able to understand what it was all about. Duncan had apparently given them the benefit of understanding English Victorian culture and all the privileges of society, including such things as the appreciation and even the performance of some of Handel's oratorios, but did not think they were capable of understanding the Lord's teaching concerning the Eucharist.

The task of going to a completely "heathen" people and attempting to take Christ to them seems an extremely difficult thing—especially if one is alone. William Duncan certainly deserves a great deal of respect and credit for his unceasing perseverance. To mould a people, who at the start were so savage that they ate each other, must have required infinite patience. These Indians were even accustomed to eating dogs raw on certain occasions as a degree of honour. It is certainly understandable that Duncan should have been fearsome that the Holy Communion might be misunderstood.

Another problem that Duncan had to face was the whole question of the "potlatch". This custom involved a person giving away certain material goods as a display. It is somewhat akin to the idea of saving face in oriental cultures. Those invited to the potlatch are then required to return the invitation (much as we expect a person to return a dinner engagement) but to outdo the previous giveaway. One can see the problems that would result. This can be seen to have both a moral and an economic aspect. Stress on personal pride and status was of course somewhat out of place in the Christian concept of life. The problem then is how is one to alter ideas and customs that have been with a people for aeons? In Tsimshean culture if a man even stumbled in public he was bound to have a potlatch in order to save face. There would obviously be many, many occasions when one would have to give away his material possessions. The social problems around the questions of poverty and property ownership, when potlatches are the norm, would be utterly fantastic. Often slaves were held to be simply personal property or chattels. They too would be traded back and forth. This situation would obviously be completely contrary to the Christian ethic and of European society's norms.

On the other hand there would be some positive factors in the converting of these Indians to the Christian faith. They did have an extremely great awareness of the supernatural. Their lives were bound up by things of the spirit. There was not the sharp demarcation between the material and the spiritual that we find in Western culture and especially in white North American culture. Also there was the advantage of working with, a people who had a very developed sense of, and love for, hospitality.

McCULLAGH OF AIYANSH

The Nass River flows westward to the Pacific and meets the ocean just north of Fort Simpson (now Port Simpson) where William Duncan had begun his activity. Approximately 70 miles up the Nass is the village of Aiyansh. It is to this place that James McCullagh, a priest of the Church Missionary Society, first came. It was in 1883 that he arrived completely unprepared for such a wild country. The two tribes that were nearby were the Gitlakdamiks and the Gitwinksilqus. They lived in villages a few miles upstream from the place where McCullagh began building his cabin and which later on became the site of Aiyansh. It is interesting to note that many of these Indian names begin with the syllable "Sit" or "Kit". This is an Indian word, which means "People of—". We find it in names such as Kitwankool, Kinkolith, and Kitimaat. While James McCullagh was building his cabin he had an accident with an axe, which caused him a great deal of discomfort and disability. He refers to this incident as his axe-i-dent. He seems to have been able to fend for himself quite admirably and reports that he was fairly comfortable in his cabin. Fresh salmon was the main item in his diet and he reports that even that delicacy can become quite tiresome. He apparently enjoyed fresh beef only once between 1883 and 1887.

In the beginning McCullagh did not believe that the Indians up the river would ever be turned to Christianity. He felt, that they were in a state of "fossilized degradation". His first efforts at preaching and teaching were very much unappreciated by the Indians and of course especially by the medicine men. The

Indians did not like the way he looked them straight in the eye when he was speaking to them. Another of his attributes that they were not fond of was that he took no abuse from them—even from the chiefs.

McCullagh, as Duncan had been, was at first obliged to be everything to these people. His first surgical operation was the repair of a finger, which had been in the barrel of a rifle when it was discharged. A certain Indian by the name of Shagaitksiwan had refused to come and hear McCullagh give his lessons and the missionary sent some men to bring him. Eventually they had to carry the man to McCullagh. However, even then he refused by placing his fingers in his ears. It was this same man who later injured himself. He had his finger in the barrel to prevent snow from getting in and a twig accidentally discharged the gun. McCullagh, half jokingly said that this certainly would prevent the man from placing his fingers in his ears when the teacher was speaking. The Indians were somewhat upset by this. They thought that McCullagh had some sort of power. At any rate it seems to have made them respect the missionary a little more.

Conversion was a very long drawn out process. The Indians were very much set on their ideas of black magic. They had a cult of spiritism similar to voodoo where a certain man of the tribe, a Necromancer, could be asked to work a spell on an enemy, which it was believed, would eventually bring about his death.

McCullagh spent long tedious hours learning the language of these people by having them tell him when he was making mistakes. The language is called Nisga'a. They did not of course have any conception of grammatical structure but they were able to inform him when they detected wrong pronunciation or order. He eventually compiled a small grammar of the language called the "Hagaga" and reduced the language to written form using some Roman letters and some Greek. He translated the Prayer Book and some hymns into Nishga. The Indians began to get quite interested in his work when he started working with a printing press. They seemed to have an unquenchable thirst for knowledge. He began to print a monthly newspaper in both languages. He also produced some of the Gospels in their language as well as periodic spelling sheets.

After his work began to have good effect and he had a body of faithful and informed Native people around him, he organized some small groups of preachers who went to the Indians in Gitlakdamiks to preach to them in their own tongue. This of course met with quite a bit of opposition at first. The heathen Indians did not know what to make of their converted tribesmen. Soon The Christian Indians began working on a road through the forest from Aiyansh to Gitlakdamiks. This road was perfectly straight and was to be used by the preachers when going to the village to preach the Gospel. The road was eventually named Gospel Road.

Fishery Bay, a centre for oolachan fishing on the Nass River, was another situation where there was an opportunity to preach the Gospel. Oolachans are a small fish from which the Indians get a thick oil or grease. It is eaten, used for cooking, put on the hair, and used for a thousand and one things. It is held to be quite valuable by the Indians. They still use it but not many of them bury it in the ground as they used to do to wait until it became ripe.

McCullagh, unlike Duncan, stressed the use of the vernacular in education. He encouraged the Indians to use their own language and to think in their own language. He taught them about other lands and tried to help them to realize that the world was much larger than they had supposed it to be. Pictures and articles were cut from magazines that he received and posted where all could see. His work as a doctor came mostly from what he had managed to read about in medical books sent out by the Society. During one particular measles epidemic he had considerable trouble with the medicine man who wanted to use the rattle over some of the patients. McCullagh simply put his foot down and refused to allow it. He told the people that if the patients died they would blame him and if they lived they would give credit to the medicine man.

Before building the church McCullagh arranged for the machinery for a sawmill to be sent. He figured that the source of building material was too far away and that they could save considerable amounts of money by making their own lumber. The machinery was brought up the river without a mishap and assembled. Unfortunately it would not work on waterpower and they had to wait until a steam generator could be brought in. Eventually this was done and the mill turned out lumber quite quickly. The church was built with the efforts of all the Indians. It was also built along with the rest of the village, at the cost of the Indians. When the church was opened there was a robed choir and everything was in order. McCullagh was actually dumbfounded at the beauty of the situation so that he could not even announce the hymn. He says he felt like prostrating himself on the floor in thanksgiving. The offering at that service was so heavy that he could not lift it to the holy table. It weighed 80 pounds and was in excess of one thousand three hundred dollars.

They had an interesting way of dealing with the offering. Since paydays were only once or twice a year for the Indians, (when they sold their salmon catch and their furs), it was not easy to deal in currency so they used 2 1/2 cent and 5 cent tickets which were purchased when the money was available and the banking was done by the warden. The Indians liked the sermons of McCullagh and were particularly attentive in church. They were very fond of any comparisons and illustrations, which were drawn from Indian Life.

McCullagh organized the people of Aiyansh as Duncan had done in Metlakatla, but he did one thing that was certainly a vast improvement. He put responsibility on other people rather than being directly in charge of everything himself. The Village Council, which was responsible for the running of affairs, was a very useful institution, which has continued to this day. In fact, the idea spread to the other villages of the Nass and they are all organized on these lines. There were people in charge of taxes, road maintenance, there was a sanitary committee which was responsible for making sure that the floors in the village houses were kept scrubbed, a Fire Master, and even a very amusing position which was called Fence Viewing—this person made sure that the fences were kept in good repair. Liquor was not allowed in the village because of the trouble, which always seemed to arise over its consumption.

The Church Army, an organization within the Anglican Church, which was modelled on the Salvation Army, was to have a place of great importance in the villages. It proved to be a real power for good and an outlet for the Indians. They would preach the gospel in the villages and in general they encouraged the cause of the faith. They had bands that were used in the open air preaching. These bands are still in existence and are surprisingly good. They are supported by an organization of women called the "Band Aid". McCullagh also organized a guild of Elders. This was for older men. They prayed with the sick and did visiting. They also made sure (or at least encouraged) that people were saying their prayers at home. The White Cross organization was a women's group that was similar to the Women's Auxiliary. They cleaned the church and conducted money-raising campaigns for the benefit of church work. Many of these lay groups that did pastoral work could very profitably be copied in the church today—in an age when we are trying so hard to involve the layman in the service of the church. The work of James McCullagh is certainly an example of the courage and devotion that is ever needed in the Christian Church.

REFLECTIONS ON DUNCAN & McCULLAGH
JULY 2012

Although initially it was not intentional, I am rather pleased to have placed this paper as the last one in the series. My reaction to reading the original essay again has had an odd double affect upon me. First, of making me laugh quite heartily at certain incidents and secondly, causing me to shed a few tears as there is so much material that evokes each of those responses as memories of the years of my ministry and people flash by. First of all, I should note that I believe I chose this particular subject from a list of church history topics principally because I was destined to go to work in the Diocese of Caledonia after ordination where these two missionaries had broken new ground in the middle of the nineteenth century.

In order to be a candidate for Holy Orders one had, in those days, to be sponsored by a bishop who, after the fulfilment of the scholastic preparation, would ordain and place him in a living or curacy in his diocese. I had met Bishop Eric Munn on several occasions and was deeply impressed with his holiness, pastoral manner, and sense of humour. He had been, in his younger days, a curate at St. James' in Vancouver and lived, as I always fantasized, in the same suite of rooms that I would one day occupy.

To be honest, there was actually another secondary and rather more mundane reason why I approached Bishop Munn for sponsorship. I discovered that there was a modest financial benefit with regard to college expenses for candidates who were destined to work in missionary dioceses. It was simply part and parcel of the life of a student who, without assistance from elsewhere, welcomed the meagre funds that waiting on tables, shelving books in the library stacks and working in northern mines and fisheries in the summer months supplied.

At the time I wrote this paper for the history component, I had not the vaguest idea that in the future I would come to have so many personal links with the early missionaries and history of the Anglican Church on the British Columbia coast.

These two gentlemen, William Duncan and James McCullagh, worked in relatively close proximity to each other, Duncan being sent first to Fort Simpson and then later serving at Metlakatla. McCullagh was involved at Aiyansh on the Naas River with the Nisga'a People. I believe they had occasion to meet from time to time to discuss their respective missions as they were both sent out under the auspices of the Church Missionary Society. In spite of that, however, they were in fact very different in temperament and in their respective approaches to involvement with Aboriginal People. Many of these nuances escaped me at the time of the writing of the college essay, but time and the experience of working with Aboriginal people on the BC coast have opened to me numerous insights.

Incidentally before I proceed any further I should note that the spelling of Aboriginal names tends to vary from time to time, I think because it makes the names more authentically native and possibly to de-Anglicize them. This practice is even more complex in the far north of Canada where places such as Baker Lake and Frobisher Bay are now called Qamani'tuaq and Iqaluit. This reminds me that since the time when I was a schoolboy using the typical 1940s atlas as a guide, I now find the world has a very different look as dozens of countries have either changed their names or have split into even more countries.

With respect to Aboriginal names, it does make it more difficult to deal with on occasion because sometimes there are orthographic symbols employed, which give them the appearance of being decidedly foreign. Undoubtedly, these changes have been made to represent more accurately sounds that are not found in English.

Duncan and McCullagh differed considerably in their basic world-views with regard to Christian belief and the ethos of the faith. Duncan seemed to relish his position of control in Metlakatla, the village he virtually created. He regimented everything to the tiniest detail and ultimately held dominion over all of it. I find it amusing that even though he believed in an essentially low church, perhaps even Calvinistic view of Christianity, he enjoyed being called Father in spite of the fact that he was not even in Holy Orders. In any case the title Father at that time would have been considered extremely Popish, and as history reveals, Duncan was quite definitely anti-clerical.

The Church Missionary Society had always been an evangelical arm of the Church. Within the limits of Anglican evangelicalism the Society strove to provide ordained clergy for their appropriate function wherever they might be and therefore they followed that principle with respect to the demanding work in the Pacific Northwest. The Rev. William Ridley was eventually chosen by CMS in England and consecrated to go to British Columbia to offer episcopal ministry to the missions on the Coast.

Duncan did not like that idea at all as it would ultimately undermine his position and control. It seems obvious that Duncan had problems with authority and quite possibly he also had personal needs that could not tolerate competition in his little kingdom. In today's parlance I think he would probably be considered a 'control freak'. His mission, it seems, was to create a Utopia, an idea that had also been attempted in any number of places down through history.

Contrasting with Duncan's approach to ministering to the residents of the Coast—a people who had lived there for aeons—was the work of James McCullagh. He embraced quite a different methodology. Instead of trying to make little

Englishmen of those amongst whom he lived and worked, he acknowledged their culture and language and was able to be amongst them as one who appreciated the harsh realities of life in the wilds of British Columbia. He made valiant attempts at assimilating with them and learning their language. I cannot really add anything significant to the old essay's account of McCullagh's history and work, except to say that I found it refreshing to read historical accounts of his work on the Naas River and to see how succeeding generations of European immigrants endeavoured to rewrite history with regard to the Church's and Government's involvement and intentions for the well-being of Aboriginal People.

Incidentally, another of the CMS priests who worked at certain times together with McCullagh was the Rev. Alfred J. Hall who eventually became identified with work at Alert Bay with the Namgis People where he founded and built Christ Church, a sawmill, a school, a salmon saltery, learned the Kwak'wala language and produced the first intricately detailed grammar of that language. I was extremely privileged to have followed him, after a long stream of others, as Rector of Christ Church where I spent a number of happy years.

For eight years before that time I had lived and worked with Aboriginal People in Northern (Arctic) Québec at Schefferville and Village de Matimekosh, Côte-Nord, and with the Blackfoot People of the Blood Reserve in South-western Alberta. During the Alberta years I lived at St. Paul's Residential School on the Reserve and served at first as Chaplain to the School as well as assistant priest at St. Paul's Church on the Reserve. I eventually became Priest-in-Charge of the Parish and continued to serve as Chaplain at St. Paul's School.

The Blood Reserve is enormous, being some 50 miles long and about 20 miles wide on the swath of land between the Belly and the St. Mary's Rivers. The school was at the very southern end of the Reserve and was a residence for students from the isolated far reaches of the Reserve. At the time I was involved it was no longer a school as such, but St. Paul's served as a residential facility from which the students were bussed into Cardston each school day to attend the provincial schools.

At some point during 2008, decades after I had worked at St. Paul's School, the Canadian Government implemented a "Truth and Reconciliation Commission" to deal with nagging problems which had gone back many years relating to the Church run government residential schools. The following excerpt is from the Government's "Truth and Reconciliation" website.

"......as part of the court-approved Residential Schools Settlement Agreement that was negotiated between legal counsel for former students, legal counsel for the churches, the government of Canada, the Assembly of First Nations and other aboriginal organizations.

The commission is an official independent body that will provide former students — and anyone who has been affected by the residential school legacy — with an opportunity to share their individual experiences in a safe and culturally appropriate manner. It will be an opportunity for people to tell their stories about a significant part of Canadian history that is still unknown to most Canadians.

The purpose of the commission is not to determine guilt or innocence, but to create a historical account of the residential schools, help people to heal, and encourage reconciliation between aboriginals and non-aboriginal Canadians. The commission will also host events across the country to raise awareness about the residential school system and its impact."

That will explain far better than I could what the Commission is supposed to be all about. Initially, I thought that it was a very good idea to finally put to rest continual wrangling about the issue of the schools. I assumed, as did most other people with whom I talked, that it would, by its very name, be modelled on the Truth and Reconciliation Commission that had taken place in South Africa when Apartheid ended. That seemed to be a very just and honest attempt to deal with problems that had so sadly plagued South Africa. In that instance, people with legitimate claims of injustice were able to meet together with the specific officials who had oppressed them. It was an opportunity for offenders to repent and express their regrets, the arrangement being that those accused would then be exempt from litigation, and for the victims to have a face-to-face opportunity to speak with those who they believed had wronged them and to hear the expected apologies and remorse. There was relatively little money granted to those who had been offended—in other words, it was most certainly not a buyout!

When the Canadian Truth and Reconciliation issue arose in the news I was glad that we had possibly come to the point when we could move ahead and experience what South Africa had done.

But, how wrong I was. The Government of Canada apparently decided that they would allocate a billion or more dollars to compensate people who claimed abuse, meaning everything from child abuse to having to learn English or having to eat porridge for breakfast and tidy up one's bed. I remember thinking to myself, My Mother used to make me eat porridge for breakfast too and she also put some strict rules into effect about my language!

I do not recall ever hearing any discussion of this process in Parliament or in the news at any time. It must have simply been a decision made by bureaucrats, and I now understand, from people who are very close to this issue that the money being talked about has already reached almost two billion dollars and the process is far from being over.

It all sounded to me like a rant about government and political speculation, but it hit me very much on a personal level one day last year. The phone rang around lunchtime one day and I was asked by a man if I was the Donald Dodman who had once worked at St. Paul's Anglican School on the Blood Reserve in Alberta. My first thought was that this must be a long lost acquaintance who was trying to contact me. Rather, it turned out to be a private investigator employed in finding people who had worked in the Residential Schools. He said he knew nothing of the situation but was simply verifying if people were still alive, and if so, where they now lived. He said that I would be hearing from the Department of Indian Affairs. That certainly gave me a rather uncomfortable chill.

As he had correctly predicted, I soon received a letter and documents from the Department of Indian Affairs. They outlined several possibilities about how I could respond to them as they had received an allegation against me from a former student of St. Paul's School. Included in the package was a photocopy of a hand-written statement from a former student who I well remember. It was appalling, disgusting and a complete fabrication. The young man had been an altar boy at St. Paul's Church—and was a person who I quite liked and held to be a friend. It very explicitly outlined in some pornographic detail a situation which seemingly involved about five boys and girls at the same time, who were involved with me in some sort of orgiastic scenario

—totally ridiculous. One statement in this allegation jumped off the page at me—"there was no penetration", hardly a phrase that a Blackfoot Indian would use, but my initial thought was, "Well, why not, as none of this is true anyway? Wouldn't that surely result in greater compensation?" Then I realized that there surely must have been a lawyer supervising the composition of this allegation and undoubtedly well aware that such a situation would necessarily lead to criminal prosecution, which was not really what they wanted to happen since that would move the whole thing into an actual legal criminal court action.

My immediate realization upon receiving this communication from Indian Affairs was that it was without a doubt some kind of kangaroo court. The instructions in the letter were that I would be able to provide a written response to the allegation, but would not be able to have legal counsel accompany me at the hearing although they did offer to pay $2500 for a lawyer to advise me beforehand if I wished it. In addition, I would not be permitted to speak during the hearing except to answer any questions the judge might have. On top of that, there would be no opportunity to meet face to face with the accuser along with the directive that I must immediately destroy the photocopy of the allegation after reading it. I thought to myself, 'This is not the Law of Canada, and I doubt that it is even legal'.

In a subsequent telephone call with the Indian Affairs person stationed in Vancouver, I made mention of the $2500 lawyer's fee and the man said, "Oh, you don't need to worry about that, it will be paid for—it's free."

I said, "It won't really be free, will it—it will come from the enormous amount of money you're throwing at these people—in fact, from the same source as your salary."

"Oh, he responded" in what sounded like a question, "you mean as a taxpayer you would be paying?"

"Of course, every Canadian taxpayer will be paying for this!"

He then very diplomatically explained to me that if I preferred, I would not be required to be present at the hearing if I chose not to—that they would simply process it. Apparently, I could opt out of having anything more to do with the situation no matter how many other allegations might happen to turn up. He gave me the distinct impression that this is exactly what they would prefer I did. I had initially been eager to participate and to defend myself.

The logistics of the hearing sounded decidedly odd to me and therefore I did choose to withdraw and have nothing to do with the process. In my middle 70s I was certainly not going to disrupt my retirement and enter into a charade like this. A good friend who also worked at St. Paul's School received many similar allegations and tried to attend and be involved with the Commission to little avail. My understanding is that many of the Blackfoot People are shocked and horrified at this exercise.

I believe that it is quite inconsistent with Canadian Law not to be able to face an accuser. I have never since heard anything from them. I would naturally be curious to know just how many other allegations might have been made against me, knowing how these things become part of the dynamic and gossip of the reserve community. But, I'm sure I never will know.

I have been in contact with several others who were staff members at St. Paul's School in those days and they have all received similar allegations, even a Blackfoot Indian who was a dormitory supervisor.

Needless to say, I do not blame the Indian People who are applying for this money, but rather blame the government, which incredulously did not have the foresight to realize what the structure of this process would bring about. Who wouldn't want to have a try at an award of from $20,000 to $100,000? A friend who listened to my passionate story remarked that she couldn't imagine any Truth or Reconciliation coming out of this process.

I have contact with people who are involved with the internal operations of the process and I have been informed that there have, as of a year ago, been well over 100,000 applications for money from the Commission and that in the end it will undoubtedly run up into many billions of dollars more. This in itself is ridiculous when one considers that during the 120 years that Canada's Residential School system was in operation somewhere around 125 thousand students ever attended the schools.

As an amusing aside, many years ago when I was in college a fellow resident was Bert McKay, a Nisga'a teacher who was doing postgraduate studies in the Education Department at UBC. Bert, years later, became very much involved with theological education on the UBC campus. Because he had come from an isolated village on the Naas River, his school years were spent at St. Michael's School in Alert Bay. On one occasion Bert remarked that those twelve years at St. Michael's had been the happiest years of his life.

✠

Although William Duncan and James McCullagh were grouped together for the purposes of my history essay they were certainly very different aside from the fact that they were both connected to the Church Missionary Society, which had sent them both off to work on the North Coast of British Columbia.

There is a very interesting aspect of the Duncan saga on which I would like now to focus some attention. It always strikes me that it is curiously pathetic how history does repeats itself. Perhaps I should say rather, how human nature tends to duplicate itself.

It is now almost a century and a half after the Metlakatla incident, and an unusually similar situation is in the process of unfolding, this time in the Diocese of New Westminster in the southwestern corner of British Columbia. Actually, it is also happening in other parts of North America and on a worldwide scale including in Britain. Fragmentation seems to be rampant everywhere in the church. It would probably be more correct to say *churches I suppose*, because it is certainly not limited to the Anglican sphere. We frequently make much of the unity that exists in the Body of Christ; that unity which is the hallmark of the Church, and yet the effects of division continue in spite of our best intentions.

In Canada, and in British Columbia specifically, the news media have had a field-day watching how the Christians love one another as they struggle, resorting even to the law courts. Civil litigation seems a rather extreme and decidedly unscriptural approach, especially for bible worshipping purists, in attempts to take buildings and property with them as they depart. Conflicts like this are often focussed on spiritual things but closer analysis suggests that it mostly boils down to questions of sexual morality or simply pure materialism. It would seem that no matter which side of the fence one happens to be on in such actions, it is undoubtedly always lawyers who are the ultimate winners.

Rumblings began to be particularly obvious in June of 2002 when the Synod of the Diocese of New Westminster discussed and debated the question of blessing same-sex unions for the third time and came to a positive vote about it.

The dissenting clergy and their lay delegates were obviously well aware that this would likely happen as someone had arranged to have the news media present so that they could televise the reaction. When the motion was passed and the Bishop had given his assent, one of the dissenting clergy made a statement at a microphone on behalf of the group and then they theatrically walked out of the assembly in protest.

I had taken retirement in 1997 and so was not present, but I saw it on the evening news that day. The result had been expected because synods in the previous two years had narrowly approved of the blessing of same-sex unions. However, the Bishop had withheld his consent because he believed the majority was too narrow even though he himself was in favour of the possibility. At the June 2002 Synod the majority vote was larger and as a result the Bishop give his consent. The result was the protest and the walking out of the dissenting clergy and laity, which represented about eight parishes or missions, most quite small but two of them fairly large. The Diocese at that time consisted of about eighty parishes.

It amazed me completely when I heard about the reaction since the church was simply endeavouring to adjust to the realities of life in this century. These same people had never made any noticeable fuss during the times a few decades ago when the church was changing its approach to remarriage after a divorce, to say nothing of the question of the ordination of women, although at that time a few disaffected groups did depart from the Anglican fold in Canada. Naturally, as seems to be typical in these situations, they claimed that they were not leaving the Anglican Church, but that the Anglican Church was leaving them. After all, in the case of divorce they certainly could have referenced a number of Jesus' own opinions about it, when he actually never uttered a single recorded word about same-sex issues.

As a member of the Diocesan Matrimonial Commission for years I recall processing dozens of applications regarding remarriage coming from some of those same dissenting clergy who were supporting members of their congregations for remarriage. Indeed, I was also aware that several of those clergy themselves were divorced and remarried.

After that fateful day in 2002 the verbal battles began in earnest. Perhaps I should specify that these were 'internet battles' because that is where most of it seemed to take place even considering the fact that the Diocese never did engage in that tawdry exercise. The dissenters were, in my estimation, quite vicious and extremely misleading in their reporting of what was happening. For instance, they continued to say, and still do, that the Bishop decided the issue, never that it was the people/synod making the decision, albeit with the Bishop's required consent.

Then in 2003 came the episcopal ordination of Gene Robinson in New Hampshire, which undoubtedly helped the dissenting Anglicans to believe that they had done the right thing. I think that the events of 2002-3 were probably the best thing that ever happened to those who dissented. Now they must have felt they finally had a genuine and valid reason to protest, while up until then their quibbling was always patently small-minded. Eventually, the group of dissenting clergy resigned from the Anglican Church of Canada and made alliances elsewhere. The story, which I have been following for these long ten years, is indeed a complex one. The worldwide Anglican story appears to be mirroring what has happened here in Vancouver, at least in a number of places, with the possible exception of Africa and the Far East.

All of this probably sounds as though it is fairly recent history having begun on a particular day in the year 2002. But it would not be true to say that, nor would it do justice to the whole complex story. I mentioned in Chapter 2 how I came to take early retirement in 1997, however, let us go back a few years—perhaps twenty or more to the time when I was working in the Diocese of New Westminster and recall how things began to deteriorate.

In order to set this in the correct time frame, I was then working in the Diocese at St. James' Parish, from June 1987 to June 1997, ten years to the day, which also included nine annual sessions of the Diocesan Synod.

Synods in New Westminster consisted of the gathering of about 350 to 400 people comprised of clergy and elected lay delegates, who would attend to the affairs and directions of the Diocese and to discuss and establish policies. During those meetings I had been clearly aware of the presence of many of those same clergy who walked out of the 2002 Synod. They were basically of the evangelical right wing and who seemed to challenge any Diocesan initiative or programme routinely. They also appeared to me to be emphatically anti-bishop. During the ten year time frame of my involvement, Archbishop Hambidge was Bishop of New Westminster and when he retired Bishop Michael Ingham became the Diocesan Bishop. This anti-episcopal attitude has truly baffled me because now those who dissent and have officially walked away from the Anglican Church of Canada seem to be preoccupied with the purple. Some wags have actually been so cheeky as to suggest that in their new, purified version of Anglicanism they have more bishops per capita than in the Church they left.

I don't believe that a Synod went by without the largest of the dissenting parishes complaining that they should be allowed to have more synod delegates because of the large number of parishioners they purported to have. The Diocese, as most dioceses do, had very specific guidelines about how many lay members, and hence votes, each parish was entitled to have. As I recall, it was something like:

Number of Parishioners	Delegates
Less Than 100	1 (+ Clergy)
100 but fewer than 200	2 (+ Clergy)
200 but fewer than 400	3 (+ Clergy)
400 but fewer than 600	4 (+ Clergy)
600 but fewer than 800	5 (+ Clergy)
800 or more	6 (+ Clergy)

Added to this is the stipulation that a delegate must be a communicant member of at least one year's standing and be at least 15 years old.

It is within the purview of each synod to establish those ratios and I know from experience that it can vary slightly from diocese to diocese. Perhaps the New Westminster numbers have changed a little since the days I was involved, but I can't imagine that it would now be very much different.

That large parish in question always seemed to be claiming to have many more people than that upper number of 800. There were also endless discussions with this parish as to why they persistently over a number of years withheld large amounts of their assessed apportionment to the Diocese. (Parish apportionment is the calculated amount of support that each parish is assessed for the operation of the Diocese based on their population and resources). They always seemed to be obstructing the work of the church in the Diocese and seemed not to really want to be part of it. To me they were blatantly saying, we don't really believe in the purposes of this church and we will do our own more authentic thing ourselves.

About half way through my ten years at St. James' I was appointed Regional Dean of Burrard. This meant that I would have certain duties in the affairs of the Diocese. On one occasion I recall receiving a census of the parishes of the diocese, which dealt with numbers, finances, ethnic groups, activities and so on. I have never been very impressed by this kind of bureaucratic endeavour, however on inspection I found the report to be extremely interesting. It was thorough and was several hundred pages long. Each parish was evaluated, obviously by some professional entity, and as I read I became more and more intrigued. I first looked at the entry for St. James' to see what they had come up with for us.

I was most impressed with the depth of the study. They had our attendance numbers, finances, staff, ethnic spread and every detail down to an amazingly accurate appraisal. I then checked out a few other parishes in Burrard Deanery with which I was familiar and found that they too were accurately detailed. So, then I turned to that large and dissenting parish to see what they were about. Without a doubt they had their financial picture accurately spelled out and their attendance numbers carefully recorded, as is customary practice for all parishes to record week by week. It evaluated properties, buildings, rectories and things all in order. But then I noticed an interesting statistic—something that quite astonished me. Most of the congregation were not Anglican in background but rather were from other denominations and the most striking statistic of all, the parish had about a 300% annual turnover rate. In practical terms that means that the average person stayed with them for about four months. Most other Anglican parishes in the Diocese had turnover numbers, which were in the teens or 20% sector presumably reflecting mobility or perhaps even the life-spans of people. In a flash of insight it dawned on me that this was really one of those mega churches where people shop around looking for God knows what, perhaps the thrill of worshipping with a large crowd, but who are certainly not particularly committed to Anglican attitudes and order. Maybe they simply enjoy worshipping with others of a like minded and overtly evangelical mindset.

That parish claims to be the largest Anglican congregation in Canada, a claim that seems to be appended to every photo or web communication and articulated repeatedly. They obviously need to believe this part of their mythology. They also claim that their history reaches back over 100 years. The parish has without a doubt been there for about 100 years but the fundamentalist sort of church it is now goes back only about 25 or 30 years. Before that time the parish was an average and typical Anglican parish. The present buildings, which are considerable, were actually built in the late 40's and were initiated by a priest, the Rector at that time, the Rev. Dr. Norman Larmonth who I well remember and who was incidentally a catholic minded Priest who in his retirement years often attended Mass with his wife at St. James'.

The parish was somehow hijacked by a fundamentalist leaning rector who was the last incumbent but one who turned the parish around into the protestant and quite unashamedly Calvinistic congregation that it is now, leaving others who did not share his views, I presume, to simply scatter and move on to other parishes or simply to give up on the church altogether. Incidentally, the Calvinistic tag, which they frequently allude to, is without a doubt the key to the whole dilemma. They are steeped in the notion that God has chosen (*fait accompli*) those who are puritans in nature and who hold to a fundamentalist view of scripture -- especially those parts that deal with their favourite issues. It is the ultra-protestant and underlying error of double-predestination which is rejected by Anglican formularies.

Incidentally, while on that particular tack I should emphasize my long held belief that the fundamentalist and puritan position is remarkably akin to the Gnostic notion of a dualistic cosmos where the realms of the Spirit and the natural, material world are at critical odds. Additionally, I believe that the current dilemma in the Church and throughout society as a whole, which so divides us are in reality a battle between the mind-sets of *exclusivity* and *inclusivity*. Jesus and the writers of the canonical Gospels clearly make the case for a Loving and All-Inclusive Creator.

The dissident clergy who walked out of Synod had before very long submitted their resignations to the Bishop and the Anglican Church of Canada. The Bishop duly acknowledged and accepted this and announced that he would be appointing clergy in their places, but at the same time he assured the people of those parishes that they were more than welcome to remain and continue worshipping in their parishes. Contrary to the often heard and blogged account of this situation, no one was ever expelled.

Perhaps they eventually panicked about their predicament and that was the point at which they collectively launched a lawsuit against the Diocese in an attempt to take the various properties along with them. The Provincial court awarded the buildings and property to the Diocese on a straightforward legal basis, as they were obviously not willing to get involved in a theological and in-house church wrangle. Then they appealed that judgement and it was also lost. Not leaving well enough alone, they then took it to the Supreme Court of Canada and lost that case as well, the Court awarding the buildings to the rightful and legal owner, the Anglican Diocese of New Westminster, along with court costs, as in each of the other attempts.

In the aftermath of that, the congregations concerned all found alternate places in which to worship and conduct their affairs, but the rhetoric about their plight still continues to announce that they did not leave the church but the church left them. This is a common meme in similar situations and has become part and parcel of their mythology. In one message on an internet site they actually referred to *their* buildings as having been '*confiscated*'. It would seem that their problem is not only with the Diocese but with the legal system as *they* themselves had initiated the court action.

Besides this, they all seem to have found African or South American bishops with whom to attach themselves or have become aligned with other dissident Anglicans all of whom seem curiously to believe that they are still under the aegis of Canterbury, even though Canterbury does not recognize them nor list them amongst the various churches of the Communion. Attempts have been made by individuals at Synods in England to have them recognized as part of the Communion, but each time their motions have been amended, reducing them to rather polite but meaningless expressions of good wishes on their endeavours.

Recently I was curious about the present day situation of William Duncan's community at New Metlakatla on Annette Island in Alaska and Googled the appropriate names. Amongst other things it brought up someone's personal web-site which included a description of their recent sailboat voyage to that part of the world. They visited New Metlakatla apparently and remarked about having seen the "William Duncan Memorial Church". They must have come across a brochure there about the history of the church, and I quote from that web-page blog: *"16 miles south you find Metlakatla which was founded by William Duncan, a missionary who had been ejected from Canada"*.

I recollect having read the history of some of the people involved in the European Reformation days in the 1530s. Specifically I recall reading correspondence between Erasmus and Martin Luther. How history does repeat itself!

Erasmus was a Dutch priest who, although he was very progressive in his thinking and even critical of many aspects of the Catholic Church, never dreamed of leaving it. He was a noted Renaissance scholar and Luther apparently fancied that Erasmus might join forces with him in his rebellion against the Church.

Erasmus had studied the classics, Greek, Latin and Hebrew and was grounded in rationalism. Examining the Roman Catholic Church, he was disappointed primarily with abuses in the Church, especially those of the clergy. These abuses are vividly and satirically described in his book, <u>The Praise of Folly</u>. He called for reform in the Roman Catholic Church and probably would have been a great asset to the Reformation, but a huge chasm separated these two men. Luther was convinced of the truth of God's word as it was revealed to him, in spite of the fact that he rejected bits of it and even had the effrontery to add things to it when he chose. He wanted true reformation in the church, which would be both in doctrine and practice. Erasmus simply wanted to promote moral reform in the Roman Catholic Church. He had no intention of leaving the Church, but remained and was supportive of the Papacy.

Erasmus was an avid correspondent and was constantly in touch with scores of people. In the letters between Luther and Erasmus, he chides and actually chastises Luther about his myopic views of scripture and was put off with Luther's notion that there was *"no pure interpretation of Scripture anywhere but in Wittenberg"*. Erasmus touches upon another important point of the controversy in another letter to Martin Luther. He remarks, *"You stipulate that we should not ask for or accept anything but Holy Scripture, but you do it in such a way as to require that we permit you to be its sole interpreter, renouncing all others. Thus the victory will be yours if we allow you to be not the steward but the lord of Holy Scripture"*. [Hyperaspistes, Book I, Collected Works of Erasmus, Vol.76, pp. 204-205.]

✠

It has been both fascinating and frustrating to watch this dissident drama unfold. The process has undoubtedly hi-lighted long festering and unaddressed issues and has done in the process untold damage to the unity of the church. I want to very briefly condense this struggle and touch on a few of the significant events and actions taken.

At various times in the 1970s Lambeth Conferences had dealt with the question of homosexuality, but in a rather perfunctory way. In 1979 the Canadian House of Bishops had ruled that ordained ministers may be homosexual but must abstain from any sexual activity. In 1985 a number of executive committee members and laypersons objected loudly to a controversial Anglican study guide on human sexuality which contained a somewhat sympathetic portrayal of homosexuals. In 1986 the Archbishop of Toronto suspended two lesbian deacons who told their congregation they were "married" and were expecting a child by artificial insemination. (I can't personally understand why they would feel the need to make that declaration).

What follows notes some of the principal moments as the issue was really beginning to heat up. The first time that any of this conflict actually came to my attention was in a news report from the 1998 Lambeth Conference. Apparently, a Nigerian bishop in the course of things, accidentally or otherwise, was introduced to the

Reverend Richard Kirker who was leader of the British Lesbian and Gay Christian Movement. He was in the vicinity of the Lambeth meetings and was distributing information leaflets. The Bishop, upon realizing what had just happened, was possibly horrified that he had actually touched Kirker's hand. He went into a fit of uncontrollable angst and shrieked in horror as he tried to exorcise demons from Father Kirker. It was during this conference that the world's Anglican bishops overwhelmingly approved a motion saying that "homosexual practice is contrary to Scripture."

The principal pivotal events of the next few years may be summarized as follows:

2002 - the Diocese of New Westminster, British Columbia, Canada, first Canadian diocese to recognize same-sex blessings.

2003 - the American Episcopal Church, the Anglican Church in the United States, appointed an openly gay man as bishop of New Hampshire.

2004 - an international panel of Anglican theologians calling for a moratorium on the blessing of same-sex unions and the ordination of gay clergy, asked the Canadian and U.S. churches to apologize for their actions.

2005 - the Anglican Primates' Meeting in Dromantine, Ireland, asked the U.S. and Canada to withdraw members from the Anglican Consultative Council.

2007 - a worldwide meeting of Anglican bishops in Tanzania demanded the U.S. Episcopalians ban gay clergy and same-sex unions by Sept. 30, 2007 or face expulsion from the Communion, which they did not do and nothing happened.

Also in 2007, Delegates at the Canadian Anglican synod in Winnipeg approved a historic motion that said same-sex blessings did not violate the *core doctrines* of the church.

2008 - the GAFCON (Global Anglican Future Conference) convened in Jerusalem and produced a Declaration. It maintained that a "false gospel" (in fact they actually called it *a different religion*) is taught by the American and Canadian Anglican Churches.

From that point to the present time:

This period—2008 to 2013—is simply so frenetic with Anglican and pseudo-Anglican activity that I am afraid I would simply not be able to do it justice nor do I really comprehend it. It is filled with mergers of separated and competing Anglican-like bodies as well as more divisions and splits—even among splinter groups—and a lot more legal wrangling. It is peppered with many acronyms, some of which are hilarious and rather appropriate. A few of them are GAFCON, which I have already noted, as well as FOCA (Fellowship of Confessing Anglicans—surely they could have left out the O for 'of' and been spared the ridicule since it is pronounced by the British like *Fokker, as in the aircraft*), TAC (Traditional Anglican Communion), and ACNA (Anglican Church in North America).

EPILOGUE

Considering the 3000 year span of the Hebrew and Christian scriptures, the 45 years between my graduate essays and my current musings upon them is but a drop in the bucket of history. Yet, it is amazing to contemplate the ideas that have developed and changed during that small fragment of time—a mere half century. It does however shed some light on one perspective—the need for those who are captivated by questions of faith and spirituality to recognize that it is essential to think and rethink our positions and beliefs.

Recognizing that there must be a willingness to allow our thinking to grow and develop is critical in order to avoid the pitfall of allowing our outlook to become fossilized. If we let that which we cherish to freeze we run the risk of preventing it from fully blossoming. On the other hand, if we permit growth and development we then give God leave to evolve in our hearts and minds. The Gospel message and principle must be treated as something that is always new, fresh, and alive leading humankind ever more toward truth and justice.

If we thwart that sort of evolution we risk hampering or even worse, completely frustrating that sacred journey and pilgrimage, which we have been called to experience and savour. Allowing God into our thinking and praying will surely leave us free to respond to the challenges and joy that lies ahead.

Κυριε Ελεησον

www.ingramcontent.com/pod-product-compliance
Lightning Source LLC
Chambersburg PA
CBHW032059090426
42743CB00007B/170